CARL ANDRE
Sculpture 1959-1977

Text by
DAVID BOURDON

Foreword by
Barbara Rose

Jaap Rietman Inc., New York

Library of Congress Catalog Card Number: 78-56827

JAAP'RIETMAN, INC.
167 Spring Street, New York, N.Y. 10012

Design by RICHARD S. HAYMES: GRAPHIC DESIGN
New York, New York
Composition by CRAFTSMAN TYPE
Dayton, Ohio
Lithography by INTELLIGENCER PRINTING
Lancaster, Pennsylvania

PHOTOGRAPHY CREDITS

Photographers are cited alphabetically,
and credits are cited by page number.

Ace Gallery, Los Angeles: 34.
David Allison: 25, 49, 53.
Geoffrey Clements: 22.
Bevan Davies: 24, 41, 45, 47, 63, 69.
Detroit Institute of Arts: 37.
Dizlo: 16, 17.
eeva-inkeri: 59.
John A. Ferrari: 65.
Ron Forth: 70.
Hollis Frampton: 8, 11.
Gianfranco Gorgoni: cover, 12, 15, 33.
The Solomon R. Guggenheim Museum: 20.
Kunstmuseum, Basel, Switzerland: 23.
David Lowe: 39.
Minneapolis College of Art and Design: 36.
National Gallery of Canada, Ottawa: 51.
Portland Center for the Visual Arts, Oregon: 38.
Dan Perlmutter: 61.
Bill Records: 88.
Renaissance Society, University of Chicago: 69.
Walter Russell: 20.

Except as specified, photographic material was
supplied by Sperone Westwater Fischer, Inc.

Cover: *Secant,* 1977, Douglas fir, 12" x 12" x 300'.
Installation at Nassau County Museum of Fine Arts, Roslyn, New York.

CARL ANDRE
Sculpture 1959-1977

LAGUNA GLORIA ART MUSEUM
Austin, Texas
7 January - 19 February 1978

THE CONTEMPORARY ARTS CENTER
Cincinnati, Ohio
2 March - 16 April 1978

THE ALBRIGHT-KNOX ART GALLERY
Buffalo, New York
8 July - 20 August 1978

THE ART INSTITUTE OF CHICAGO
Chicago, Illinois
9 December 1978 - 14 January 1979

LA JOLLA MUSEUM OF CONTEMPORARY ART
La Jolla, California
2 February - 18 March 1979

UNIVERSITY ART MUSEUM
Berkeley, California
9 May - 24 June 1979

DALLAS MUSEUM OF FINE ARTS
Dallas, Texas
18 July - 3 September 1979

MUSEE D'ART CONTEMPORAINE
Montreal, Canada
15 October - 23 November 1979

INSTITUTE OF CONTEMPORARY ART
Boston, Massachusetts
7 January - 17 February 1980

CONTENTS

Carved wood sculptures, New York, 1958-1959.

"The imagination must be given not wings but weights."   Henry Adams

A RETROSPECTIVE NOTE   by Barbara Rose

Looking back to the day in 1956 when I first met Carl Andre, I recall a young man whose ruddy cherubic face was crowned with a stubby crewcut fringe— he had just been mustered out of the U.S. Army—a young man of uncommon wit and a talent for literature and poetry so original it bemused John Crowe Ransom, his teacher before Andre's expulsion from Kenyon College. Coupled with these engaging qualities was a great embracing generosity, in particular toward persons of the opposite sex, and an ingenuous disregard for the material world, or what some might call "reality." For Carl was among the unregenerate who continued and, so far as I know, continues to place the pleasure principle above the reality principle.

Even at that early date, Carl was immersed in the life of the mind; whereas I was devoted to its opposite, the pursuit of graduate degrees in art history. Yet we found much in common, as, for example, our mutual feeling that the real hero of our time was not Willem de Kooning, but George Metesky, the Mad Bomber. Together with our little band of insurrectionary young spirits, so many of whom have ascended to positions of then undreamed of establishment success, we roved through the bars and taverns, the movie houses and sleazy transient hotels of the Upper West Side. Even in such company, Carl stood out; he was the first and possibly the last Renaissance Man I ever knew. He was prolific in the extreme, producing exotic works in all media. He wrote in many genres: satirical novels, which became ever more abbreviated until they were but a paragraph in length, anticipating the contemporary attention span, as well as concrete poems with words arranged in symmetrical grids, as his metal plates would later tile the ground with neat adjacent squares.

Unshackled by inhibition, Andre improvised cacaphonous atonal piano music and conceived of unperformed and unperformable operas and epics. In playful moments (indeed I never knew him to have any others) he wrote lyrics to mock pop tunes with lines like "Art and Nature never goin' to rendez-vous so rock with me baby and we'll rock the whole night through." And he was famous as a bearer of such epigrams as "Many are the wand bearers; few are the true bacchanals" or as a solution to war, "Let them eat what they kill."

It was about this time that Andre began calling me "Varya," my name in Russian, which led me to believe that he had been reading texts on Constructivism. On the other hand, he may simply have called me Varya because he did not know the Polish word for Barbara. In an endless stream of creativity, Andre drew and painted, experimenting with spices as redolent pigment, dreaming of "negative sculptures" whose forms were incised within solid blocks of transparent plexiglass. A few of these survive, although Andre could not afford to produce many on his salary as a brakeman on the Pennsylvania Railroad. However, it was before his tenure with the railroad that Andre first became involved with the fundamental, irreducible definitions of making and constructing. I first saw Andre's wood pieces in 1959. After an unfortunate accident in 1964, in which Andre, who had been promoted to a freight conductor, caused several trains to nearly collide, he was quite ready to accept E. C. Goossen's invitation to reconstruct one of the large sculptures I had seen earlier.

There are times when I ask myself if it was Andre's intention all the time to become a hero of official culture by combining Courbet's overalls with Monet's beard. In retrospect, I think not. We are all the product of our own peculiar historic moment, and Andre's moment was one in which every challenge to prevailing orthodoxies was instantly convertible into an amusement, a diversion, a spectacle, as television for example could transform the Vietnam War into a dinner-time action serial.

As we measure integrity by continuity, we can trace the thread of integrity in the continuity of Andre's pursuits. Absurdity, especially historical absurdity, is the stuff anarchism feeds on; the attraction of anarchism for artists is precisely its capacity to treat the inexorable logic of totalitarianism, in its various guises, with the illogic of the arbitrary and the unruly. In this connection, one of Andre's most consistent features is arbitrariness, our sense that the rules of the art game are entirely of the artist's capricious design, which will inevitably confront the varieties of dictatorships of taste or decorum.

One may perceive, or that is I perceive, a connection here between Andre's interminably reiterated modest and less modest proposals and the anarchistic character that came to dominate late Suprematist-Constructivist thought after the Revolution when, as a result of Lenin's withdrawal of support from the avant-garde, artists had to choose between the extremes of nihilistic conceptualism—the affectless dematerialized Idea—and utilitarian productivity—geometric jumpsuits or elegant typography in the service of the State. Confronted with similar alternatives, Andre chooses a third thing: to make works that are both substantially material as well as good for nothing, structures that imply building but cannot house.

To say that Andre's works are good for nothing is perhaps to exaggerate. In fact, they may no longer aspire to transform the world, but they certainly exist to criticize it. In common with Constructivist ideals, Andre employs standard, frequently mass-produced modules which are arranged in mathematically determined structures. One may also connect his philosophical investigation of the rudiments of fabrication—its relationship to hand as well as machine craft—and his desire to make art directly accessible to the masses to ideas latent in Constructivist thinking.

The idea that Andre's art is in essence democratic might seem perverse; yet he, like Ad Reinhardt who claimed that "This is your painting if you paint it" holds forth the possibility of Andre for everyone. Certainly Andre's stacks of

Styrofoam, rows of bricks, metal squares, and piles of timber are more literally available to the layman than Reinhardt's meticulously applied and carefully mixed shades of black. Andre displays the raw materials with which we could transform the world, if we cared to build a new order.

In his generosity, Andre shares his pure Idea with the world: This is your Carl Andre if you want it. The "surplus value" attributed to his conception by the museological industry is the invention of the economic system into which Andre's ideas find their way. Redefining the terms of "making" as neither industrial fabrication nor handicraft, but the work of the mind insisting on its supremacy over matter, Andre hints at a world in which the imagination dominates. Our knowledge that his structures cohere through juxtaposition rather than being bolted, nailed or welded together in the manner of utilitarian or even previous sculptural construction puts them in an alien sphere. We know that Andre's works exist only while we perceive them; but they are more than the literal proof of Bishop Berkeley's theories concerning the relationship between perception and existence.

Dismantled, stacked, stored, they regain their identity as mundane modules. In returning to their original state after their "death" as artworks, Andre's art follows the rule of nature. They reflect in the inevitability of their fate a world that is no longer stable, static and firmly connected, but mobile, transitory and held together by fragile and mutable relationships. Like Marcel Duchamp, Andre first assumed and then unshakably maintained a radical polemical stance in the world, which has for the most part chosen to use his work for its own purposes. Nevertheless, Andre's art remains both a criticism of a world that refuses to understand its message, as well as a continuing challenge to search for new solutions to an impasse operating at every level. Inert but not inexpressive, Andre's structures parallel the human condition: their lease on life is as provisional, as tenuous, and as fugitive as our own.

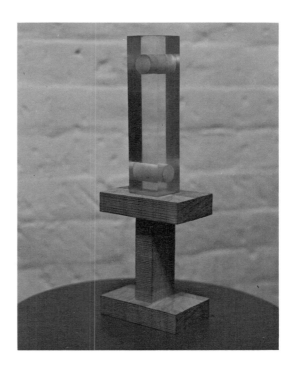

Maple and Plastic Exercise, 1959, wood and plastic, 12" x 2½."

A REDEFINITION OF SCULPTURE
by David Bourdon

Carl Andre's investigation of sculpture as "place" has possibly resulted in the most drastic redefinition of three-dimensional art in the last 40 years. His terse account of the evolution of 20th-century sculpture from "form" to "structure," and from "structure" to "place" helped explain what was original in much Minimal sculpture and helped determine the character of a great deal of art made since the mid-'60s[1] The implications of his definition were important for the development of earthworks and many other pieces, both outdoors and in, which interact significantly with their environments.

But Andre is more than an ideologue, and the first to disqualify himself as a Conceptual artist, though he is clearly an important source for the Conceptual movement. He is, first and foremost, consciously extending the traditions of modernist sculpture. Though decision-making plays an unusually large role in all of Andre's work, he always gives equal importance to its materiality. "My works are not the embodiments of ideas or conceptions," Andre once said. "My works are, in the words of William Blake, 'The lineaments of Gratified Desire."[2]

Andre's sculpture can be categorized in numerous ways, but four characteristics are notably persistent:

1. Flatness. Andre often seems to deprive sculpture of one of its traditional dimensions — height. The vertical dimension of many of his floor pieces is as low as ⅜" and even less. In such cases, the work is virtually two-dimensional, suppressing any suggestion of spatial illusion. By making sculpture of unprecedented flatness, Andre also dispenses with any overtones of anthropomorphism. Traditionally, most sculpture refers, however obliquely, to a body, human or otherwise, which has an outside and an inside. David Smith's ostensibly abstract, totemic constructions, for instance, not only allude to the human body, but also mimic a human stance. Andre, by contrast, eliminates any hint of inner

Left to right: *Lever,* 1966, Firebrick. The National Gallery of Canada; *Well,* 1964/1970, Wood, Wallraf-Richartz Museum, Ludwig Collection; *Pyramid,* 1959/1970, Wood. Installation at the Solomon R. Guggenheim Museum, 1970.

space and, like a steamroller, demolishes all anthropomorphic references.

2. Modular composition. Andre's sculpture generally consists of standardized materials, used as untransformed elements in a repetitive manner. The identical units—which may be bricks, metal plates or timbers—are usually positioned in linear or square configurations directly on the floor or ground and left unjoined. Gravity alone holds the elements in place. The arrangement is non-hierarchical; that is, no part differs from or has more importance than any other part. All units are the same, and may be interchanged within each configuration.

3. Generic space. Andre refers to his art as "post-studio sculpture" since he devises most new work for particular exhibition sites. The setting is considered an integral part of the work, and the form of each piece is largely determined by the space for which it is initially constructed. While Andre prefers to work with a particular location in mind, he is most mindful of scale. "I don't think spaces are that singular," he says. "I think there are generic classes of spaces . . . So it's not really a problem where a work is going to be in particular. It's only a problem, in general, of the generic spaces: is it going to be the size of Grand Central Station or is it going to be the size of a small room?"[3]

4. Use of ordinary materials and forms. Andre does not invent new materials, techniques or shapes; to the contrary, he simply arranges ready-made or "found" materials in simple geometric configurations. "My particles," he said, "are all more or less standards of the economy, because I believe in using the materials of society in the form the society does not use them."[4] His forms and materials are available to almost anyone. Everybody's six-year-old child, that proverbial *wunderkind,* could probably recreate an Andre work and the replica would be indistinguishable from the original. Andre's apparent lack of invention is methodical and deliberately intended to focus our attention on the materials, the way in which they have been ordered and their setting.

Two of Andre's most characteristic works are *64 Steel Square* (see page 55) and *Secant* (see cover). The first, made in 1967, consists of 64 steel plates, eight inches square, laid down like unjoined tiles in a square grid. The gestalt and materiality of the work are immediately apparent. There is no suggestion that the piece is any more than what it appears to be. The sculpture does not significantly change as we circumambulate it. Andre's decisions in composing the work are also self-evident: eight-inch modular particles are laid down in a square of eight rows of eight plates each. But the work holds the floor in a compelling way, functioning as a kind of zone within a larger space. Visually, the piece begins to come alive as we notice discrepancies and differences from one square to another; the various scratches, marks and variations in color and surface texture assume an almost autographic quality. If we stand on the piece it tends to slip away in our peripheral vision, while the disconcerting way in which the tiles sway under our feet persuades us that the sculpture is not as stark and inflexible as we may have first imagined.

Secant, made ten years later for a group show at the Nassau County Museum of Fine Arts on Long Island, is a 300-foot-long line of Douglas fir timbers, each 12 x 12 x 36 inches. Spectators, strolling on the museum's wooded grounds, suddenly encountered one end of *Secant* atop a grassy knoll; from there, the work descended into a rolling meadow surrounded by trees. Like a spine, it articulated the sinuous rise and fall of the land, while introducing a new scale into the natural setting. Because an actual secant is a straight line, cutting a curve at two or more points, Andre's *Secant* is both the undulating line of timbers and the straight sight line connecting its two ends. *Secant* was one of the latest and longest in a series of essentially linear pieces that the artist has made since 1966, the year he exhibited the 34½-foot-long row of firebricks,

Secant, 1977, Douglas fir, 12" x 12" x 300'.
Installation at the Nassau County Museum of Fine Arts, Roslyn, New York.

Quincy: Family grave.

Quincy: Andre's boyhood home.

Lever, which generated tremendous controversy at that time. *Secant* is a far more seductive work than *Lever,* possessing greater beauty in its flowing line and more potential complexity in relation to its site.

Andre repeatedly declares that his ideal piece of sculpture is a road. "Most of my works—certainly the successful ones—have been ones that are in a way causeways—they cause you to make your way along them or around them or to move the spectator over them. They're like roads, but certainly not fixed point vistas. I think sculpture should have an infinite point of view. There should be no one place or even a group of places where you should be."[5] *Secant,* which suggested a section of paths, certainly fulfilled this requirement, offering a constantly varying perspective to spectators walking alongside it.

Because Andre deals only with known, commonplace forms and does not transform his materials, he is often viewed with skepticism by the general public and certain groups within the art world. To spectators who cannot comprehend how ordinary bricks and metal plates can suddenly assume an identity as "art" simply because a self-proclaimed artist has moved them from one place to another, Andre's work exemplifies the Emperor's New Clothes. Even some otherwise sophisticated art-world people see it as pure put-on.

Andre's candor about his work does not always pacify his audience. During the furore over his *Stone Field Sculpture* in Hartford, a newspaper reporter noted the following exchange between the sculptor and passersby. "How can we be sure you're not putting us on?" the spectators asked. Andre replied, "I may be putting myself on. If I'm deceiving you, then I've deceived myself. It's possible."[6]

Andre, like any artist, has been influenced to some extent by everything that has entered into his experience. But his sensibility has been most strongly affected, or confirmed, by a relatively small number of persons, structures and places, ranging from Constantin Brancusi, Gertrude Stein, Ad Reinhardt and Lao Tzu to Stonehenge, Russian Constructivist art, Japanese temple gardens, the Pennsylvania Railroad and Quincy, Massachusetts.

Quincy, where Andre was born on September 16, 1935, is an austere, historically minded city, immediately south of Boston. To Henry Adams, who spent his formative years in Quincy during the second quarter of the 19th century, the city was in many ways a poor cousin to Boston. "Though Quincy was but two hours' walk from Beacon Hill," Adams wrote, "it belonged in a different world."[7] More importantly: "Quincy had no Boston style."[8] In lieu of style, Quincy had epic granite quarries, famous even in Adams' day. When Adams wanted

Quincy: Abandoned quarry.

Quincy: Memorial works.

to make a metaphor about a particular type of education, he compared it to seeds falling "on the stoniest soil in Quincy, which is, as everyone knows, the stoniest glacial and tidal drift known in any Puritan land."[9] Andre grew up amid this severe terrain, and one of his earliest memories of landscape concerns the quarries, particularly at night when large granite prisms were silhouetted against the moon. "But even more, the Quincy of my boyhood was a city of tidal waters, creeks, bays, marshes, islands and shipyards with their giant girders and cranes and acres of flat steel plates lying in the weather."[10]

Andre is the youngest of three children and an only son. His father's people are of Swedish descent, the men in the family tending to be in the building or metalworking trades. His grandfather was bricklayer and his granduncles were blacksmiths. Andre's father, a retired marine draftsman, is an accomplished woodworker with a cellarful of power tools. He lives in a house he designed and built himself, even down to the ironwork hinges and latches on the cabinets. Andre's mother, who is of Scottish descent, awakened his interest in literature and music.

From 1951 to 1953, Andre attended Phillips Academy in Andover, Massachusetts, where, among other things, he studied art with Maud and Patrick Morgan. In 1954, he traveled to England, where a maternal aunt and uncle guided him through many historic sites, including Stonehenge and other megalithic monuments. Andre was greatly moved by the elemental simplicity of the ancient stones and their cryptic deployment on the land; references to Stonehenge surfaced in Andre's art several years after this visit. On this same trip, Andre visited Paris and the Louvre.

Andre settled in New York in 1957 and took a job as a production assistant with a textbook publisher in order to subsidize his activities as an artist and poet. Through Hollis Frampton, a friend and Andover roommate, Andre met Frank Stella, who had moved to Manhattan from Princeton in 1958 and supported himself by working as a house painter. A year later Stella began turning out austere paintings of black stripes in his tiny second-story loft on West Broadway and Broome Street, in what later became Soho. The three young men shared food and drink, exchanged ideas, inspired and criticized each other's work.

Frank Stella's keen intellect made a strong impression upon Andre, who came to regard him as a kind of teacher. Stella, who is several months younger than Andre, had also attended Andover, but the two artists did not meet until both lived in New York. Stella's success was almost immediate. His series of large Black paintings quickly roused the interest of a small group of admirers, who were entranced by his somber arrangements of stripes into binary, cruciform and concentric symmetries. Four of these Black paintings were selected for inclusion in "Sixteen Americans," an important exhibition at the Museum of Modern Art in 1959. Because few critics were lined up behind Stella in those days, he asked Andre to write a statement for him in the catalogue. Andre supplied a terse manifesto: "Preface to Stripe Painting. Art excludes the unnecessary. Frank Stella has found it necessary to paint stripes. There is nothing else in his painting. Frank Stella is not interested in expression or sensitivity. He is interested in the necessities of painting. Symbols are counters passed among people. Frank Stella's painting is not symbolic. His stripes are the paths of brush on canvas. These paths lead only into painting."[11]

Andre's own mode of visual expression was shifting from two dimensions into sculpture. His early works were in wood and reflected the influence of both Stella and Brancusi. Andre was more attracted to Brancusi than to any other 20th-century sculptor because the Romanian master was unexcelled at essentializing forms. Andre also concurred with Brancusi's notion that direct cutting is somehow superior to modeling. The young American was particularly impressed by Brancusi's carved wooden bases with their repetitive motifs and by his *Endless Columns,* the tallest of which rises nearly 100 feet high in Tirgu Jiu, Romania. Andre's carved beams were repeatedly notched in a modular fashion that evoked both Brancusi and Stella. One day in 1959, Stella pointed out the uncut, "back" surface of Andre's *Last Ladder* (page 20) and remarked that it was sculpture, too. From that point, Andre came to realize "The wood was better before I cut it than after. I did not improve it in any way."[12] The wood beams or, for that matter, whatever material he chose to work with, he realized, already had a strong sculptural presence. Years later he observed: "Up to a certain time I was cutting into things. Then I realized that the thing I was cutting was the cut. Rather than cut into the material, I now use the material as the cut in space."[13]

Andre's renewed perception of positive and negative space was reinforced by a reading of the *Tao Te Ching,* a compilation of wise sayings, traditionally ascribed to Lao Tzu, an older contemporary of Confucius. This text places considerable importance on "nothing," i.e., empty space:

"Thirty spokes share one hub. Adapt the nothing therein to the purpose in hand, and you will have the use of the cart. Knead clay in order to make a vessel. Adapt the nothing therein to the purpose in hand, and you have the use of the vessel. Cut out doors and windows in order to make a room. Adapt the nothing therein to the purpose in hand, and you will have the use of the room. Thus what we gain is Something, yet it is by virtue of Nothing that this can be put to use."[14]

Having determined that he would no longer cut into or otherwise alter his materials, Andre embarked in 1960 on his Element Series, consisting of standardized, 12 x 12 x 36 inch timbers, arranged in simple, orthogonal configurations. Some, like *Tau and Threshold* (page 49), allude to classic architectural forms, while one, *Herm* (page 47), consists only of the basic unit. Since Andre had neither the money nor the space to realize these works, they existed only in the form of "proposals," graph-paper drawings that he showed to potential sponsors. No one volunteered to support the project, one dealer fearing that the unjoined state of the timbers would endanger his clientele.

In retrospect, Andre believes it was a good thing he did not exhibit the Element Series at that time, since he would not have known how to follow them up. Even if he had shown them, they might have gone unremarked, since the prevailing mood in the 1960s art world was still expressionist. Though the inclusion of Frank Stella, Jasper Johns, Ellsworth Kelly and Jack Youngerman in the "Sixteen Americans" show signaled the rise of more rational, clearly structured painting, most of the acclaimed sculptors of the period were making assemblages and "junk" sculpture, soon to be endorsed by the Museum of Modern Art's "Art of Assemblage" show in 1961. The prevailing excitement over "new media" and "new forms," such as the rhetorical scrap constructions of John Chamberlain and Mark di Suvero, both admired by Andre, assured that hardly anyone would be interested in anything as reductive and conservative as a set of squared timbers. Andre was not aware at the time that his proposals had historic antecedents, specifically in Alexander Rodchenko's 1920 *Construction of Distance,* consisting of several units of square timbers stacked in orthogonal relationships to make up a kind of open cube. When he later realized the similarity, he immersed himself in studies of Russian Constructivist art.

The early 1960s were difficult, confusing years for Andre. In order to support himself and his wife, Andre took a job for four years as a freight brakeman and conductor on the Pennsylvania Railroad. When he was not engaged by

Constantin Brancusi, *Endless Column,* 1918, Oak, 80″ x 10″ x 9⅝,″
Mary Sisler, Palm Beach, Florida.

Carl Andre, *Last Ladder,* 1959, Wood, 84½″ x 6⅛″ x 6⅛,″
The Tate Gallery.

the railroad, employed in local service in northern New Jersey opposite Manhattan, he was at home on the Lower East Side, making art that was antithetical to what he had done before. In place of the purist forms, which previously occupied him, he now turned out rather revolting assemblages, incorporating broken glass, old clothing, doll parts, cigarette butts and artificial roses; most of these works were destroyed soon after.

Andre devoted more time than usual to his writing, searching for new poetic forms. Unlike his earlier, relatively lyric poetry, his new poems were "shaped"; that is, the words—usually nouns—were marshaled in orderly, nongrammatical patterns. For instance, he once arranged dozens of words into vertical columns, aligned flush to the left; the opposite side automatically had a serrated edge since Andre had chosen alternating words of three, four and five characters. The regularly notched gestalt of the poem obviously alluded to his carved beams. The spatial intervals are as important as the words in Andre's poetry, and the overall shape or gestalt of the poem encourages us to look at it as a design rather than read it for sense. The poetry takes varied forms: typed on white paper, hand printed on graph paper, or scissored from printed matter and collaged. Andre has produced a substantial body of such works, and continues into the present to turn out poems, "operas" and occasional books, which could easily be the subject of an entire essay.

Writers on Andre are generally tempted to draw parallels between his experience with the Pennsylvania Railroad and his subsequent sculpture. It is certainly easy to understand how his taste for regimented, modular components might have been affirmed by the interchangeable freight cars and the evenly spaced railroad ties. The rails and ties could have helped persuade him that his sculpture should be horizontal, parallel to the earth, rather than standing, totem-like, upon it. The adaptability of the track to its terrain and the convergence of two or more lines in particular locations undoubtedly sharpened Andre's perception of "place." The artist acknowledges his railroad experience as a strong influence on his work. Whatever he learned in the rail yards, Andre emerged a much better sculptor.

In 1964, the art writer and educator Eugene C. Goossen organized an exhibition of "8 Young Artists"—all emerging Minimalists—for the Hudson River Museum in Yonkers, New York. Goossen remembered being impressed by Andre's wood pyramids, which he had seen four years before in Hollis Frampton's apartment, so he invited the artist to exhibit. Unfortunately, the tenant who took over Frampton's apartment had used the pyramids for firewood. As a result, Andre reconstructed a work now titled *Cedar Piece* (page 23) consisting of 19 tiers of notched, interlocking lengths of wood, each 36¼ inches long. Unlike the original, which had been made of 2 x 4" fir, the new version is 4 x 4" cedar, giving it a more massive appearance. Each of the four elevations of *Cedar Piece* is identical, a stepped progression of modular elements that is symmetrical from side to side and from top to bottom. On each of the four sides, the ends of the beams constitute an X-shaped configuration, which, when viewed from an angle, creates the illusion that the work is indented at its midsection. The serrated contours and internal symmetries relate to Frank Stella's stripe paintings, while the overall structure implies a potential continuation, as in Brancusi's *Endless Column*. Though *Cedar Piece* alludes to Stella and Brancusi, it remains one of Andre's most original authoritative early works.

Andre's first exhibition in a New York City art gallery took place the following year at the Tibor de Nagy Gallery in a group show, called "Shape and Structure." Like Goossen's show, "Shape and Structure" focused attention on younger artists who practiced a style that came to be known as Minimalism. Throughout the early '60s, the Minimalist impulse became increasingly evident,

Frank Stella, *Die Fahne Hoch*, 1959, Enamel on canvas, 121½" x 73", Whitney Museum of American Art, New York: Gift of Mr. and Mrs. Eugene Schwartz and purchased through the generosity of Mr. Peter Brant, The Lauder Foundation, The Sydney and Frances Lewis Foundation, Philip Morris, Inc., Mr. and Mrs. Albrecht Saalfield and the National Endowment for the Arts.

Opposite: *Cedar Piece*, 1959/1964, Cedar, 36½" x 36½" x 68¾". In background, Frank Stella, *Morro Castle*, 1958. Both: Collection Kunstmuseum Basel.

particularly at the Green Gallery, which exhibited the work of sculptors Robert Morris, Donald Judd, Dan Flavin and painters Ralph Humphrey and Tadaaki Kuwayama. The de Nagy roundup featured ten of the more innovative painters and sculptors of that time, including Judd, Morris, Larry Bell and Walter Darby Bannard. Andre's contribution was a massive structure, *Well* (page 12), which consisted of 28 12 x 12 inch timbers, each three feet long, stacked in a square seven rows high to make a closed hexahedron. This structure is large enough to contain a standing human body, but its solid walls of large timber had the effect of aggressively excluding the spectator, who felt literally up against a wall. It was a massive, almost domineering piece and, compared to the elegantly detailed glass and plexiglass boxes by Bell and Judd, had an almost brutish presence.

A few months later, Andre mounted his first one-man exhibition at the Tibor de Nagy Gallery. As he explained later: "I wanted very much to seize and hold the space of that gallery—not simply fill it, but seize and hold that space."[15] Large timber pieces would have been too heavy for the gallery floor, which had threatened to buckle under his "Shape and Structure" contribution, so Andre sought a material with high volume and low mass. A friend suggested he investigate Styrofoam and this lightweight plastic turned out to be ideal. Andre pur-

Pyre (Element Series), 1960/1971, Western red cedar, 36" x 36" x 48".
The Gilman Collection, Jacksonville, Florida.

Opposite:
Page from Carl Andre's 1960 drawing book of the Element Series.

chased several dozen Styrofoam slabs, which were manufactured in nine-foot lengths, and arranged them in three different configurations. Their titles—*Coin, Compound* and *Crib* (page 26)—referred to building terms. Sixteen of the white plastic beams were stacked to make *Coin,* a right-angled wall with a quoined corner angle. *Compound* was a two-foot-high solid wall, penning in an open square. The largest, most impressive piece was *Crib,* a square, latticed structure, enclosing 500 cubic feet of space.

Collectively, the Styrofoam works, which so jammed the gallery that spectators had to maneuver with care, were a startling conclusion to Andre's sculpture-as-structure. While he would continue to stack and align materials, he would find ways to do so that did not evoke architecture. Like some of his earlier works, the plastic pieces suggested primitive building forms, being essentially vertical and employing positive/negative spatial relationships. While he could have continued in this direction, which many viewers found absorbing, Andre chose to make more forceful cuts in space, uncompromised by ambiguous inside/outside, positive/negative distinctions. Instead of building structures to "seize and hold" space, he wanted to destructuralize his work and use materials in a way that would be place-generating.

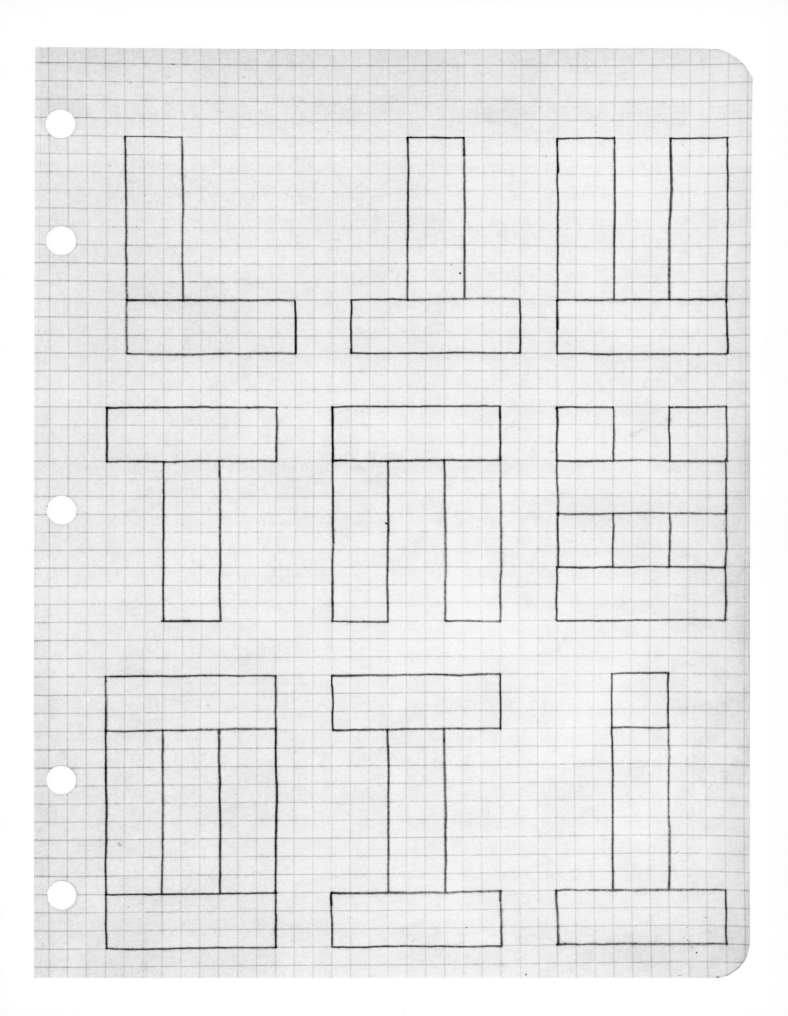

During the summer of 1965, Andre experienced a revelation while canoeing on a New Hampshire lake. He had long wanted to break away from the vertical in his sculpture, and it now suddenly occurred to him that his work should be as level as water. He wondered how he could go about putting the equivalent of Brancusi's *Endless Column* on the ground instead of in the air. His initial — and instantly controversial — solution was *Lever* (page 51), which he designed the following February for an important sculpture show at the Jewish Museum in New York.

Lever was a work of unprecedented flatness in Andre's *oeuvre*. It also was one of the most startling contributions to the "Primary Structures" exhibition at the Jewish Museum; the show was a comprehensive survey of geometric constructions, much of them in large scale and in bright colors, made by 42 "younger" American and British sculptors, and it emphatically established the importance of Minimal sculpture, though that name was not affixed to the movement until the following year. Many of the artists in the exhibition had abandoned the notion of sculpture as "form" (and some of them much earlier than Andre), but many were preoccupied with the concept of sculpture as "structure" and, consequently, the museum was filled with regimented cubes, slabs and cones.

Crib, Coin, Compound, 1965, Styrofoam beams.
Installation at the Tibor de Nagy Gallery, New York, 1965.

Lever, which consisted of 137 unjoined firebricks, extended along the floor for 34½ feet; one end abutted a gallery wall, the other approached a doorway. The piece was designed for a specific space, so that viewers in two neighboring galleries would have distinctly different views of it. From one adjoining gallery, viewers who looked through the doorway saw a segment of the work in elevation, extending horizontally like a horizon line. From the second entranceway, viewers met the piece head-on, seeing it in receding perspective. "All I'm doing," Andre said at the time, "is putting Brancusi's *Endless Column* on the ground instead of in the sky. Most sculpture is priapic with the male organ in the air. In my work, Priapus is down on the floor. The engaged position is to run along the earth."[16]

Lever jarred its audience for a number of reasons. As sculptural material, the firebricks seemed uncommonly humble, and the artist had obviously applied no visible craftsmanship in aligning them in a row. The linear form appeared singularly uninventive and undynamic. Compared to two of the biggest crowd-pleasers in the exhibition — Ronald Bladen's untitled trio of canted, aluminum-and-wood slabs and Robert Grosvenor's suspended 31-foot-long *Transoxiana* — Andre's piece involved relatively little mass and consumed a modest amount of space, yet proved disconcertingly assertive. For some irritated viewers, *Lever* was uningratiatingly literal, lacking too many of the conventional properties of sculpture. The bricks struck some spectators as a belated example of Dada, reminiscent of Marcel Duchamp's designation of certain "found objects," such as a urinal or shovel, to be works of art. The major difference is that Duchamp chose and put into an art context individual manufactured objects, the shapes of which had been determined by their use. By contrast, Andre's units are the basic materials of construction and manufacturing. A few people were put off by the seemingly arbitrary number of bricks, believing that the piece would not change substantially with the addition or subtraction of a dozen or so bricks. Others were annoyed, surprisingly, because the work appeared unsalable; they theorized that since anybody could purchase similar bricks and assemble an identical work, nobody would buy the original.

Happily, *Lever* not only polarized its audience, but also prompted many people to reexamine their assumptions about sculpture. There was the issue of flatness to ponder. There was renewed interest in the properties of materials, and the questions of whether the artist should impose new properties, alter existing ones, or simply leave things as they are. Andre obviously made the latter choice, evidently feeling it would be presumptuous to alter the existing color, surface or shape of his materials. Instead, he preferred simply to reveal their inherent properties. The bricks particularly appealed to him because of their compressed mass and uniform composition. *Lever's* bricks were not physically transformed, yet they were denied their usual function as building units. Bricks are common to several civilizations, and were used to build structures even in prehistoric times, but Andre's bricks elude architectural connotations since they are neither stacked nor joined. Using another material, such as glue, to bind the elements of his works strikes him as being somehow false and limiting.

"The materials I use have been processed by manufacture," he said, "but have not been given the final shape of their destiny in the manufacturing culture . . . I wouldn't ever be interested in laying a brick wall with mortar." Andre believes that by leaving his units unjoined, he leaves their potential free. "If my work has any subject matter at all, it is the immense potentiality of the things around us."[17]

Lever, in addition to being uncommonly flat and composed of unaltered, unjoined materials, exemplified Andre's concept of sculpture as "place." It was

Equivalents I-VIII, 1966, Sand-lime brick.
Installation at the Tibor de Nagy Gallery, New York, 1966.

perhaps the only work in the "Primary Structures" exhibition specifically made for the space it would occupy. While Dan Flavin, Robert Morris and Donald Judd and others had earlier made sculpture that was interdependent with its architectural setting, Andre placed even more importance on the overall character of the surrounding space. According to him: "A place is an area within an environment which has been altered in such a way as to make the general environment more conspicuous."[18] He later revised this definition: "Placing is cutting into space. Place is the finite domain of one or more cuts into space."

That same spring, in his second one-man show at the Tibor de Nagy Gallery, Andre showed related brick pieces that he conceived at the same time as *Lever.* Each of the eight floorpieces consists of 120 bricks, stacked in two identical layers. Consequently, every layer has 60 bricks, aligned along their stretcher or header axis to constitute various rectilinear shapes in four out of six possible combinations: 3 x 20, 4 x 15, 5 x 12 and 6 x 10. Each permutation appeared in two possible variations, depending on whether the bricks were aligned along their short or long axis. The same 6 x 10 combination, for instance, can be both an elongated rectangle or a near square.

Andre titled the series *Equivalents,* after the renowned cloud photographs made by Alfred Stieglitz in the 1920s and '30s. Stieglitz intended his cloud images to demonstrate that his success as a photographer was not due en-

Cuts, 1967, Concrete block capstones, 2″ x 368″ x 512″.
Installation at the Dwan Gallery, Los Angeles, 1967.

tirely to subject matter. Clouds are, after all, freely available to everyone. He succeeded in achieving striking, evocative images that are simultaneously literal and poetic, verging on abstraction. It would be an exaggeration to say that Andre's installation suggested that Stieglitz's amorphous, evanescent clouds had somehow condensed into heavy, concrete matter, but the sculptor's *Equivalents* demonstrated again that an artist with superior perception can convert commonplace subjects and materials into arresting works of art.

The eight floorpieces collectively established an austere, contemplative environment, comparable to certain Japanese temple gardens. None of the works adjoined the gallery walls. Instead, the pieces were dispersed across the floor, like randomly spaced platforms. Individually, the pieces seemed impersonal, cool and aloof, but not intimidating, since they were so low (less than six inches). Each *Equivalent* had the same mass and volume, yet visibly differed, underscoring the discrepancy between what we intellectually know and actually see.

As a kind of counterpart to his *Equivalents* exhibition, Andre devised a reverse installation, titled *Cuts,* for the Dwan Gallery in Los Angeles in March 1967. He installed a single layer of concrete block capstones across the floor of a 30 x 42 foot gallery, leaving eight, rectilinear negative openings, or "cuts," which corresponded to the positive shapes and positioning of the *Equivalents* at the de Nagy Gallery. This demanding work was not without its ambiguities. Were the eight depressions in the concrete "floor" to be viewed as "cuts," or was the layer of brick itself the cut in space? The *Equivalents* were eight different works, while *Cuts* appeared to be a single piece with eight major compositional elements, all voids. In eliminating almost every possible reference to form and structure, Andre succeeded in creating an allover "place." *Cuts* was visually severe and physically disconcerting for gallery-goers who were unaccustomed to walking on loose, slightly wobbly blocks, let alone on a work of art. Some unwitting spectators did not accept the artist's implicit invitation to join in the space of the piece; they took one look at the cement floor, thought the gallery was being renovated and hastily retreated.

Cuts was the closest Andre came to making "negative" sculptures, cavities below floor- or ground-level. The implications of this piece were realized a little later by some of the makers of earthworks, while Andre himself chose to keep his cuts-in-space above ground level.

For Andre, the late 1960s were a period of continued experimentation, involving magnetism, gravity, organic and inorganic particles, irregular particles and random arrangements. In 1966, he made several magnet floorpieces which are notable for their relatively small grids and miniscule height (half an inch or less). They also differ from his other modular floorpieces in that their surfaces are exceptionally taut, the magnetic force squeezing out the interstitial space between units. That same year, he also produced a scatter piece, called *Spill,* consisting of 800 small plastic blocks, collectively dumped from a canvas bag onto the floor and left to assume their own random configuration. Though Andre adhered, as usual, to geometric units, he let gravity do the arranging, the process remaining self-evident in the final result. He again incorporated gravity when, in the spring of 1967, he devised a *Monument for a Small Child,* as his contribution to a group show, "Monuments, Tombstones and Trophies," at the Museum of Contemporary Crafts. From the second-floor landing, Andre poured a bag of sand onto the main floor, the sand forming a small, conical mound. In theory, a corpse buried under a full-scale pile of sand would disintegrate into dust by the time the sand has blown away. It was more of a poetic gesture than anything else, but this transient "tombstone" was a memorable example of the type of "antiform" or process art that was just beginning to emerge, as many artists began to let their materials assume more "natural" shapes.

In 1968, he devised a temporary outdoor piece for Windham College in Putney, Vermont, consisting of a row of hay bales aligned side by side along the ground to produce a 274½-foot-long causeway, extending from a graded field into a forest clearing. He called it *Joint* to signify its connecting of two different types of space. The hay, normally pliant, was compacted into stiff, solid modules, a man-made form as geometric as a brick or ingot of metal, but subject to relatively fast decomposition. That same year, in Aspen, Colorado, he made another, less successful outdoor work by throwing rocks together into a 10-foot diameter pile. Andre was not particularly satisfied with these works. "My most successful works are those made of uniform elements," he said. "I had not been able to make a work of irregular elements which was really satisfactory until *Stone Field Sculpture.* My scatter pieces, except for some sand ones, were unsuccessful attempts to make small pieces from small elements."

Andre continued to explore different types of "places," those that exclude and a great many more that implicitly invite the spectator to enter into or onto them. Since his unjoined, interchangeable units can be stacked up and stored away, Andre was able to reuse the Styrofoam beams from his 1965 show in a new work, called *Reef* (1966). In their new configuration the beams were aligned on edge, side by side, extending nine feet into the room, along an entire wall of the Park Place Gallery. He referred to this work as a kind of plateau, "a place of no access."[19] In 1969, he reconstructed a larger version of this work for "Anti-Illusion: Procedures/Materials," an exhibition at the Whitney Museum.

Unlike *Reef,* which excludes viewers from occupying its space, Andre's metal floorpieces, which he began making in 1966, may be walked upon. Andre does not intend that *all* his sculptures be stood upon; the Styrofoam beams, for instance, would not survive pedestrian traffic. For those works that are suitable for being walked on, the artist recommends that spectators enter them and stand in the middle. He speculates that viewers can distinguish the different materials under their feet. "I believe that man is equipped with a subtle sense of detecting differences in mass between materials of similar appearance but with different mass," he said[20] "Standing in the middle of a lead square would give you a sense entirely different from standing in the middle of a square of magnesium." Andre also relishes the possibility that the spectator who walks across the sculpture may not even see it. "You can stand in the middle of it and you can look straight out and you can't see that piece of sculpture at all because the limit of your peripheral downward vision is beyond the edge of the sculpture."[21]

Spill (Scatter Piece), 1966, 800 plastic blocks (approx.) and canvas bag, John and Kimiko Powers, New York.

Collectors, understandably, may be apprehensive about the cumulative effect of footsteps upon a work of art, but, according to Andre, it's all part of the piece. "My works are in (a) constant state of change. I'm not interested in reaching an ideal state with my works. As people walk on them, as the steel rusts, as the brick crumbles, as the materials weather, the work becomes its own record of everything that's happened to it."[22]

The largest and most complex of Andre's floorpieces is *37 Pieces of Work,* designed in 1969. The work consists of 36 Plains, each six feet square, laid side by side in rows to form an overall sculpture that is 36 x 36 feet. The constituent squares are called Plains rather than "planes" to emphasize their geographic role as "place" rather than to call attention to their flat, geometric surfaces. The 37th "piece" is the collective entity.

As installed on the floor of the Guggenheim Museum during Andre's one-man show there in 1970, *37 Pieces of Work* was a dazzling, metallic array of foot-square plates of aluminum, copper, steel, magnesium, lead and zinc each ⅜ inch thick. Each metal was used alone to constitute one 36-unit square, then alternated checkerboard fashion, with each of the other metals, thus demonstrating the possible permutations. The metals were installed in the alphabetical order of their chemical symbols: Al, Cu, Fe (the symbol for iron of which steel is the most common alloy), Mg, Pb and Zn.

Viewed from the museum's spiraling ramp, *37 Pieces of Work* resembled an intricately patterned field. While the whole thing looked like an eccentric, multicolored gameboard, spectators could easily sort out its constituent elements and subsets. All six Plains on one side of the work were monochrome, since each consisted of a single metal. Aluminum predominated in the six Plains along another side, while zinc prevailed on the remaining two sides. In addition to the clustering of metallic hues in various sections, there were frequent changes in rhythmic intervals wherever two plates of the same metal abutted each other in neighboring Plains. Collectively, the 1,296 metal plates provided a lively staccato quality, as syncopated, emphatic and intricate as the small rectangles of color that seemingly dart along vertical and horizontal axes in Mondrian's celebrated Boogie Woogie paintings. In contrast to the building's high, domed space, sinuous curves and cream-colored walls, *37 Pieces of Work* was flat, angular and shiny, holding its own within Frank Lloyd Wright's *tour de force.*

Andre's Guggenheim retrospective featured fewer than three dozen sculptures, but was sufficiently varied to indicate how much ground he had covered in only 12 years. Though the show was generally well received, the consensus seeming to be that the metal floorpieces were particularly compelling, some viewers began to fret about what Andre would do later. Or, rather, what he *could* do. As it became apparent in the early '70s that the Minimalist school, if not its leaders, had lost momentum, critics increasingly wondered if Andre hadn't tile-set himself into a corner.

Jeremy Gilbert-Rolfe speculated that Andre was now "confronted with the problem of maintaining a position based on an ultimate reduction . . . The problem that Andre now faces isn't one of an inability or reluctance to change, but its opposite, the possibility that change will undermine the main thrust of the work, and turn it into a more traditional enterprise."[23]

Roberta Smith declared that "the severe reduction of Andre's sculpture has left him few alternatives for development. He cannot change too much without undermining the power of his original statement, and thus it becomes a position which is more ideological than esthetic, something like the one Ad Reinhardt occupied: admirable, uncompromising and uncomfortable."[24]

The aesthetic quality of Andre's sculpture is scarcely noted by some critics,

37 Pieces of Work, 1969, Aluminum, copper, lead, magnesium, steel, zinc, ⅜" x 432" x 432".
Installation at the Solomon R. Guggenheim Museum, 1970.

who tend to see it as demonstrating ideas or ideology. Peter Schjeldahl, for instance, wrote that "Andre's message seems more ethical and social than esthetic. That is, his work seems to exist less as something to be enjoyed than as an embodied proposition about what art *ought* to be. His is an aggressive, even truculent sensibility. In its simultaneous obtrusiveness and reluctance to please, his art might almost be saying something like, 'Take that! It's no less than you deserve!'"[25]

Considering the severe limitations Andre has set on his sculpture since 1965, the wonder is that he continues throughout the '70s to find ever new ways to elaborate and extend his original themes. He succeeds in developing as an artist without undercutting his initial premises about flatness and standardized, unitary elements. He has, to be sure, produced some rather ordinary series, such as the Copper Cardinals and the Decks, which predictably revive earlier motifs. To my mind, many of the flat, linear pieces lack visual presence, being too insubstantial physically to hold the floor with much authority. But he has devised more successful, visually lush series, such as the Triodes, the Uncarved Blocks and the Copper Corners.

Each work in the Uncarved Block series consists of two to five 36-inch beams of western red cedar, positioned on the floor so that one beam stands vertically, while others, referring to the four points of the compass, lie horizontally at right angles to its base. The orthogonal configurations and the color and surface of the wood give these pieces a lively warmth.

Both the Copper Corner and the Triode series are made of flat copper plates, each 50 centimeters square. Thanks to the rich color and shimmer of the copper, the pieces are relatively showy and alluring. The metal is reflective, throwing dappled pink-orange-rose-colored light onto neighboring walls; the reflected light becomes a partial mirror-image, implying the continuation of the work into surrounding space. The Triodes feature one row of square copper plates, aligned parallel and adjacent to the wall, with another row extending orthogonally from the center and probing into the room. The shape is similar to a "T," the top of which abuts the wall; but all three axes are the same length and equidistant from the center plate. Consequently, the copper "path" that projects into the room is only half as long as the line along the wall. Unlike the square Plains, which tend to establish finite zones, the Triodes more dynamically incorporate the surrounding empty floor with the wall serving as backdrop. The name

Uncarved Blocks, 1975, Western red cedar.
Installation at the Ace Gallery, Los Angeles, 1976.

"triodes," borrowed from electronics, combines the Greek words "tri" (three) and "hodos" (path or way). The Copper Corners (page 61) are essentially triangular floorpieces laid flush against the walls of a corner with a serrated hypotenuse that seemingly fans out into the room.

Andre also has made special installations for specific sites in Minneapolis, Detroit, Hartford and many other cities. In 1976, he designed *Prime Leaves* (page 36) for the Minneapolis College of Art and Design. This temporary out-door installation consisted of modular, rusted-steel plates, aligned in fifteen progressively longer rows, projecting from the base of a wall. The components in each row represented the succession of prime numbers from one to 43. The irregular spaces between the rows indicated the intervals of non-prime, or composite, numbers. A similar formula underlay the design, that same year, of *Prime Terrane* (page 37), a 36 x 55 foot work made for the Detroit Institute of Arts. *Prime Terrane* was a plaza-like groundwork, consisting of 4,872 dolomitic cement blocks, stacked in one to three layers to create a predominantly level surface that had fourteen linear depressions on one side and an equal number of linear protrusions on the opposite, all resembling the configuration of *Prime Leaves* in both negative and positive relief.

Numbers play an important role in Andre's work, though he is quick to point out he is neither a numerologist nor a mathematician. "My competence in mathematics is a value that tends perpetually to approach zero, but never quite arrives. I am only an appreciator of mathematics in the sense that we were taught musical appreciation in grade school. But neither am I a believer in the magic of numbers, anymore than I am a believer in the magic of poetry."[23]

Andre is recurrently attracted to prime numbers, possibly because of their individuality and their irreducibility. His linear pieces often consist of units that constitute a prime number. Andre feels the linear pieces have to be prime numbers in order to maintain their integrity as lines, because composite numbers with factors other than themselves and one might imply rectangles. The more factors in a number, the more possibilities for shapes. Certain numbers strike Andre as squares or triangles. For instance, 36 suggests to him both a square and a triangle because it is the square of six and the sum of all numbers from one to eight.

"The useful properties of numbers are that they succeed each other, one after the other, and that they can be told apart," he said. "Some numbers are products of equal factors (squares, cubes, etc.) and other numbers are products of only themselves and one (primes). The first count squares (2 x 2, 3 x 3, 4 x 4...), the second count lines (1 x 2, 1 x 3, 1 x 5, 1 x 7...). Other numbers are the sums of consecutive numbers beginning with one (1 + 2 + 3 + 4 + 5 + 6 + 7 + 8 = 36) and count triangles."

One of Andre's most beautiful, if untypical, works in recent years was the *144 Blocks and Stones* (page 38) installation in 1973 for a 120 x 50 foot space at the Portland Center for the Visual Arts in Oregon. The work atypically in-volved the stacking and mixing of materials—individual riverbed stones and mineral specimens centered alternately on foot-square cement blocks, ordinarily used to pave patios. Andre initially planned to use only the cement blocks, but, on outings around Portland, he found himself collecting smooth river stones, which he picked up for free, and buying science museum specimens of Oregon's minerals, from pumice and gold ore to vermiculite, argillite, acti-nolite, peridotite and pyrite. Back at the Portland Center, he arranged the patio blocks into eight rows of 18, leaving three-foot intervals between rows. He hand-sorted the river stones and then positioned them by size in a series of nesting, L-shaped rows, which alternated with L-shaped rows of the mineral samples. The piece harmoniously juxtaposed natural and man-made materials

Prime Leaves, 1976, Steel.
Installation at the Minneapolis College of Art and Design, 1976.

and evoked a fanciful cemetery in which the cement blocks became grave markers, the stones and mineral specimens being ritual offerings.

Despite his persistent emphasis on the importance of site in determining his sculpture, Andre seldom availed himself of the opportunity to create outdoor works. He made relatively few outdoor pieces, and all were temporary—until 1977, when he created *Stone Field Sculpture* (page 39) for downtown Hartford. *Stone Field Sculpture* consists of 36 boulders, weighing from 1,000 pounds to 11 tons, laid out in eight progressively smaller rows. Andre positioned the biggest boulders in the narrowest angle of the triangular site, a city-owned green that is approximately 290 feet long by 53 feet wide. Starting from row "one," which has only one very large boulder, each subsequent row has an additional stone; that is, the fourth row has four stones, the fifth row has five, and so on. The longer the row, the smaller the boulders. Also, starting from row "one," each successive line of stones is spaced progressively farther apart. To a spectator near the eight-boulder row, the distant stones appear as if seen through a telephoto lens, because they are, in fact, spatially compressed.

Prime Terrane, 1976, Dolomitic cement blocks, 8″ x 36′ x 55′.
Installation at the Detroit Institute of Arts, 1976-1977.

The boulders vary considerably not only in size, but also in color and surface, being sandstone, brownstone, granite, schist, gneiss, basalt and a greenish rock known as serpentine. Andre selected the boulders at a Bristol, Connecticut gravel pit, similar to those he had known as a youth in Massachusetts. He chose the stones for their size, shape and color, but made most of his aesthetic decisions in determining how they should be placed. He decided to employ natural boulders, rather than standardized, manufactured products, because they typified New England's glaciated landscape. To an observer, the boulders have a weight, durability and stability that seemed appropriate for an insurance capital like Hartford.

Stone Field Sculpture was inspired in part by the Colonial tombstones in the Center Church graveyard, which adjoins the green. It also developed from the artist's use of graded riverbed stones in the *144 Blocks and Stones* installation he made for the Portland Center for the Visual Arts. The Hartford piece has some of its origins in Andre's 1954 visit to Stonehenge and other megalithic monuments in England. Though he has not visited Carnac on the Brittany coast, he is aware of the menhirs there, hundreds of upright stone slabs that extend in eleven parallel rows along the shore. Andre's *Stone Field Sculpture*

144 Blocks and Stones, 1973, Concrete blocks, river stones and geological specimens. Installation at the Portland Center for the Visual Arts, Oregon, 1973.

deliberately evokes funereal connotations and heightens an awareness of the vast discrepancy between human and geological time. It is one of Andre's most tranquil, meditative "places."

•

In retrospect, the evolution of Andre's art appears almost linear and predictable. But in fact, his stylistic development was neither constant nor easily inferred from past experience. Only the artist himself can know how many false starts and how much backtracking interfered with his seemingly smooth progress; and only he can be aware of the number of contradictions that beset him along the way. "I believe that when I stop contradicting myself, I will have started to tell lies."[27]

Andre deliberated long and hard at every stage of his renunciatory art, and the result is an *oeuvre* of exceptional strength and vitality. Several of his sculptures are classics of the Minimalist mode and represent a drastic culmination of the reductive impulse — an impulse that did not originate full-blown with the Minimalists of the '60s, but which had been developed and honed by numerous predecessors, ranging from Malevich and Mondrian to Rothko, Newman and

Stone Field Sculpture, 1977, 36 glacial boulders, 290' x 53', Hartford, Connecticut.

Reinhardt. The further minimalization, or essentializing, by artists of the '60s was achieved mainly in terms of eliminating metaphysical references and emphasizing a more empirical kind of rationality.

Andre's originality and his contribution to the reductive aesthetic is already a historic, certifiable fact. Originality and quality are not synonymous, however, and at times even antithetical. The enduring quality of Andre's work will be determined later by others. For myself, I can only admire the stringent clarity of the sculpture, its commanding visual presence and stark, forthright physicality. The works strike me as concrete distillations of a unique, contemporary sensibility.

1. Andre's provocative outline was first published in this form:

   "The course of development:
       Sculpture as form
       Sculpture as structure
       Sculpture as place"

   It initially appeared in an article by David Bourdon, "The Razed Sites of Carl Andre: A Sculptor Laid Low by the Brancusi Syndrome," *Artforum*, October 1966, pp. 14-17; the text is reprinted in *Minimal Art: A Critical Anthology*, edited by Gregory Battock, E.P. Dutton & Co., Inc., New York, 1968, pp. 103-8.
2. *Carl Andre*, exhibition catalogue, Kunsthalle, Bern, 1975, p. 5.
3. Phyllis Tuchman, "An Interview with Carl Andre," *Artforum*, June 1970, p. 55.
4. *Carl Andre*, exhibition catalogue, Haags Gemeentemuseum, 1969, p. 6.
5. Tuchman, *op. cit.*, p. 57.
6. Diane Henry, "Some Residents of Hartford Are Throwing Stones at Sculptor's Extended 'Serenity of the Graveyard,'" *New York Times*, September 5, 1977, p. 21.
7. Henry Adams, *The Education of Henry Adams*, edited by Ernest Samuels, Houghton Mifflin Co., Boston, 1974, p. 9.
8. Adams, *op. cit.*, p. 10.
9. Adams, *op. cit.*, p. 14.
10. All Carl Andre quotations for which no source is given were made in conversation or correspondence with the author in 1977.
11. *Sixteen Americans*, The Museum of Modern Art, New York, 1959, p. 76.
12. Enno Develing, Essay in *Carl Andre*, exhibition catalogue, Haags Gemeentemuseum, 1969, p. 39.
13. Bourdon, *op. cit.*, p. 104.
14. Lao Tzu, *Tao Te Ching*, translated with an introduction by D.C. Lau, Penguin Books Ltd., Baltimore, 1963, p. 67.
15. Tuchman, *op. cit.*, p. 61.
16. Bourdon, *op. cit.*, p. 104.
17. Sandy Ballatore, "Carl Andre on Work and Politics," *Artweek*, July 3, 1976, p. 1.
18. *Carl Andre*, exhibition catalogue, Haags Gemeentemuseum, 1969, p. 5.
19. Tuchman, *op. cit.*, p. 61.
20. Tuchman, *op. cit.*, p. 57.
21. *Ibid.*
22. *Carl Andre*, exhibition catalogue, Haags Gemeentemuseum, 1969, p. 5.
23. Jeremy Gilbert-Rolfe (review), *Artforum*, June 1974, p. 68.
24. Roberta Smith (review), *Artforum*, January 1976, p. 62.
25. Peter Schjeldahl, "One Takes Away, the Other Piles It On," *New York Times*, April 29, 1973, II, p. 21.
26. Carl Andre and Hollis Frampton, "On Certain Poems and Consecutive Matters," unpublished manuscript of March 3, 1963 conversation.
27. Carl Andre, interviewed by Jean-Claude Lebensztejn, *Art in America*, July-August 1975, p. 71.

Stone Field Sculpture, 1977, 36 glacial boulders, 290' x 53', Hartford, Connecticut.

WORKS IN THE EXHIBITION

1. *Pyramid (Triangular Plan)*
   New York 1959 (destroyed)/
   Orleans, Massachusetts 1977 (remade)
   Pine
   69" x 31" x 31" overall
   G.H. Andre, Orleans, Massachusetts

This work, initially made in 1959, is one of the artist's earliest constructed, as opposed to carved, sculptures. It is fabricated from standard materials — in this case, 74 pieces of 2 x 4" pine, each 31" long. The overall shape, however, still suggests a carved form. The serrated contours refer directly to the sculptural forms of Brancusi's *Endless Column*. Andre's wood stack is also indebted to Frank Stella's early paintings, in which black stripes are starkly regimented across the canvas. In fact, Andre began constructing his *Pyramid* series in Stella's New York studio, using a radial saw to notch the wood; but he did not complete the triangular piece at that time. The present version was reconstructed in 1977 by the artist's father, George Hans Andre.

2. Herm (Element Series)
New York 1960 (proposed)/
New York 1976 (made)
Western red cedar
1 vertical timber
12" x 12" x 36" overall
Angela Westwater, New York

Andre considers the Element Series to be the first works in his mature style. Each work consists of 12" x 12" x 36" timbers, arranged in various orthogonal configurations. Several pieces in the series suggest basic architectural forms, primarily posts and lintels. Unlike the earlier *Pyramid (Triangular Plan)*, the wood units in the Element Series are not notched or cut. Instead of cutting into his materials, Andre used them whole as "cuts in space." *Herm* consists simply of the fundamental unit of the series. Its shape and erect stance are inescapably anthropomorphic. The title derives from the ancient Greek road markers known as Herms, square stone pillars surmounted by a bust of Hermes. Andre designed the Element Series in 1960, but because of lack of funds, did not realize them until 11 years later.

3. *Tau and Threshold (Element Series)*
   New York 1960 (proposed)/
   New York 1977 (made)
   Western red cedar
   3 timbers, 1 vertical centered on 1 horizontal
   and supporting 1 horizontal beam parallel to base
   12" x 12" x 36" each
   12" x 36" x 60" overall
   The artist

This symmetrical structure is virtually two-dimensional, like a linear drawing in space. The three beams are placed in right-angled relationships to each other in the tradition of Mondrian, who earlier advocated the use of only horizontal and vertical axes. Though the timbers are stacked in a vertical configuration, the two horizontal beams suggest twin horizon lines, underscoring its relationship to the ground. The title refers to the architectural form that lies under the door and to the Greek letter "T" (tau).

4. *Lever*
   New York 1966
   Firebrick
   137-unit header course (1 x 137)
   2½" x 4½" x 8⅛" each
   4½" x 8⅛" x 34½' overall
   The National Gallery of Canada, Ottawa

This was one of the most severely reductive works in the 1966 "Primary Structures" exhibition, which helped establish the Minimal school in New York. Designed for a specific space within the Jewish Museum, the floorpiece extended 34½ feet from the base of a wall across most of a gallery. It was the first of Andre's works to create public controversy. It remains among his most important sculptures because it embodies many of his sculptural characteristics such as horizontality, modularity of components and the spatial articulation of an existing environment. The row of 137 firebricks constitutes not only an exceptionally low sculpture, but also eliminates any vestige of internal space. Andre chose to use bricks because they impressed him as clastic, in the sense that they are unmalleable fragments or particles. Unlike materials that can be shaped plastically, Andre's inflexible units can only be arranged. He chose the particular number of firebricks because it is a prime number, having no factor other than itself and one. *Lever's* title refers to a rigid bar used as a simple machine as well as the French verb "to raise."

5. *Equivalent VII*
   New York 1966
   Sand-lime brick
   120-unit rectangular solid, 2 high x 6 stretcher x 10 header
   2⅝" x 3¾" x 8" each
   5½" x 38⅝" x 48" overall
   Manuel and Jane Greer, New York

This is one of a series of eight works initially exhibited at New York's Tibor de Nagy Gallery in 1966. Each consists of 120 bricks, stacked two high in four different rectangular formats: 3 x 20, 4 x 15, 5 x 12 and 6 x 10. There are two visibly different versions of each configuration, one with the bricks aligned along their short (header) axis, the other along their long (stretcher) axis. The works are large enough to create a feeling of "place" and sufficiently reposeful to establish a mood of placidity. Their titles are derived from Alfred Stieglitz's series of cloud photographs, also called *Equivalents.*

Equivalent VIII, the other 6 x 10 configuration, inspired controversy in London in 1976, when newspapers ridiculed the Tate Gallery's purchase, for $12,000, of "a pile of bricks." The popular press and even the ordinarily thoughtful *Burlington Magazine* denounced the Tate for squandering public money on something that might have occurred to any bricklayer. As a result of this belated notoriety, which occurred 10 years after the piece was created, *Equivalent VIII* suddenly became one of the Tate's biggest attractions.

6. *64 Steel Square*
New York 1967
Hot-rolled steel
64-unit square (8 x 8)
⅜" x 8" x 8" each
⅜" x 64" x 64" overall
Jan and Ingeborg van der Marck, West Lebanon, New Hampshire

One of the artist's early works in a square format, this sculpture is also flatter than most of its antecedents. Andre's first large metal floorpiece consists of steel plate, already cut into squares, which he purchased from a salvage company on Canal Street in downtown Manhattan. The proportions are typical of Andre: he frequently squares the size of the module (in this case, 8") to arrive at the overall size (64" here).

7. *Lead-Copper Plain* (illustrated)
   New York 1969
   Lead and copper
   36-unit square (6 x 6), 18 plates
   each metal alternating
   ⅜" x 12" x 12" each
   ⅜" x 72" x 72" overall
   Albright-Knox Art Gallery,
      Buffalo, N.Y.
   Charles Clifton Fund

8. *Zinc-Copper Plain*
   New York 1969
   Zinc and copper
   36-unit square (6 x 6), 18 plates
   each metal alternating
   ⅜" x 12" x 12" each
   ⅜" x 72" x 72" overall
   The artist

9. *Lead-Magnesium Plain*
   New York 1969
   Lead and magnesium
   36-unit square (6 x 6), 18 plates
   each metal alternating
   ⅜" x 12" x 12" each
   ⅜" x 72" x 72" overall
   The artist

10. *Steel-Steel Plain*
    New York 1969
    Steel
    36-unit square (6 x 6)
    ⅜" x 12" x 12" each
    ⅜" x 72" x 72" overall
    Columbus Gallery of Fine Arts
    Columbus, Ohio

These works are four of the 36 square Plains that constitute *37 Pieces of Work,* (see page 33) created by Andre for his one-man exhibition at the Guggenheim Museum in 1970. Each Plain consists of the 36 metal plates in a 6 x 6 array and all 36 Plains are joined together in a 6 x 6 square to form a sculptural ensemble with overall dimensions of ⅜" x 36 x 36 feet. Taken as a whole *37 Pieces of Work* consists of 1,296 plates, 216 each of aluminum, copper, steel, magnesium, lead and zinc. Each metal appears alone in individual six-foot square Plains, then alternates with another, checkerboard fashion, in every possible permutation. Since each of the six metals in the large piece was laid out in the alphabetical order of its chemical symbol, alternating successively with the others, there are two versions of each combination. Consequently, there are six monometal and 30 bimetal Plains. The 37th "piece" is the whole ensemble, as exhibited at the Guggenheim.

Among the four Plains included in this exhibition, *Zinc-Copper* is attended by electrical overtones, since it is the electro-chemical properties of these dissimilar metals that made possible the voltaic cell, an 18th-century landmark in the development of current electricity. The juxtaposition of these two metals, both known and used in prehistoric times, result in one of the brightest, warmest-looking Plains. *Lead-Magnesium Plain* in two shades of gray, contains the heaviest and lightest of the six metals used by Andre in the large work. Magnesium weighs .06 pounds per cubic inch, while lead weighs .41 pounds per cubic inch. The artist believes that viewers walking across or standing on the piece can detect the almost seven-fold differences in the specific gravities of the two metals.

11. *Seven Steel Row*
    New York 1975
    Steel
    7-unit line extending from base of wall
    ½" x 24⅛" x 17⅞" each
    ½" x 24⅛" x 125⅛" overall
    The artist

Like *Lever,* this work consists of a linear sequence of units that constitute a prime number, the pathlike shape extending from the base of a wall into the room. Andre frequently positions his sculptures projecting from a wall, believing that this orientation reduces the possibility of future confusions about subsequent sitings of the work. The rectangular steel plates in *Seven Steel Row* were "liberated" by Andre while scavenging at an excavation site in Manhattan.

12. *Twelfth Copper Corner*
    New York 1975
    Copper
    78-unit corner extending from base of wall in corner
    0.5 cm x 50 cm x 50 cm each
    0.5 cm x 600 cm x 600 cm overall
    The artist

This piece, in plan, is a right triangle with its 90-degree angle laid flush against the walls of a corner, the serrated hypotenuse projecting into the room. The ambiguous title refers not to the numerical position of this work in a sequence of related pieces, but, instead, to the fact that there are 12 copper squares in each row along both walls. In other words, Andre started out in the corner, laid down a row of 12 squares along one wall, returned to the other wall and laid down an adjacent row of 11 squares, succeeded in with rows of 10, nine and so on, until he reached the final row with only one square. The radiant, shiny surface will alter in time, due in part to the scuff marks left by spectators, many of whom like to position themselves in the corner, which affords a radial view of the triangular floorpiece, and due even more to the air, which tends to induce a greenish, carbonate coating. The *Twelfth Copper Corner* was initially designed at the request of the Whitney Museum for its mammoth 1976 exhibition, "200 Years of American Sculpture"; but the artist withdrew the piece before the show opened because the museum director refused to install the sculpture in the agreed-upon space for which it was intended.

13. *The Way North, East and South (Uncarved Blocks)*
    Vancouver 1975
    Western red cedar
    4-units, 3 horizontal pointing north, east and south
    adjacent to the base of 1 vertical
    12" x 12" x 36" each
    36" x 48" x 60" overall
    The artist

Andre made the Uncarved Blocks series for a 1975 show in Vancouver, British Columbia. The 15 works in the series consist of 12" x 12" x 36" timbers, the same size as the wood units in his earlier Element Series. Like the Elements, the Uncarved Blocks present the timbers in both vertical and horizontal axes, but never stacked. All the works in the Uncarved Blocks series feature a single vertical element. The variations occur in the number and position of the adjacent horizontal units. The horizontal timbers refer to the four points of the compass, while the vertical element alludes to the fifth point of the Chinese compass: the location of the observer.

The Uncarved Blocks series was inspired in part by the *Tao Te Ching,* an ancient Chinese text and the principal document of Taoist thought. The concept of an "uncarved block" is a recurrent motif in the *Tao Te Ching,* a metaphor with many implications. The Taoist "uncarved block" is an innocent, almost childlike state where there is limited knowledge and freedom from desire. It possibly symbolizes the original condition of man. It is also a tranquil state to which worldly people can revert if they submit themselves to the Taoist way toward virtuous conduct.

Western red cedar is a fragrant, straight-grained, unusually durable wood that is prized for its ability to withstand decay. The Northwest Coast Indians used western red cedar for their totem poles and canoes. Though the wood is being milled today, it will not survive much longer as a commercial species. It requires 200 to 250 years for a western red cedar tree to fill out to commercial size, making it uneconomical for the timber industry. Instead of reforesting cutover areas with such a slow-growing tree, timber companies substitute Douglas fir, which yields a commerical tree in about 40 years.

14. *144 Tin Square*
New York 1975
Tin
144-unit square (12 x 12)
⅜" x 12" x 12" each
⅜" x 144" x 144" overall
The artist

This is the seventh in a series of 12-foot square floorpieces, consisting of foot-square units of a single metal. The first six preceded *37 Pieces of Work.* The aluminum, steel and zinc squares were made in 1967, the copper, magnesium and lead squares in 1969. Despite their uniform dimensions, the works in this series vary considerably in surface, texture, weight and cost, tin being the most expensive. The first six works of the series are owned by major museums: Aluminum, Pasadena Art Museum; Copper, the National Gallery of Canada; Steel, Hessiches Landesmuseum, Darmstadt; Magnesium, The Tate Gallery; Lead, The Museum of Modern Art; Zinc, the Milwaukee Art Center.

15. *Seventeenth Copper Cardinal*
   New York 1977
   Copper
   17-unit line extending from base of wall
   0.5 cm x 50 cm x 50 cm each
   0.5 cm x 50 cm x 850 cm overall
   The artist

Like *Lever* and *Seven Steel Row,* this work extends from the base of a wall and consists of repeated modules that constitute a prime number. Like the *Twelfth Copper Corner, Seventeenth Copper Cardinal* will continue to have its color and surface altered by weather and use. Andre's Copper Cardinal series, initiated in Italy in 1973, consists of square plates arranged in linear, rectangular and square formats. The prime numbers are linear, while composite numbers are always rectangular and sometimes square. The Copper Cardinal with the largest number of units, so far, is *Eighty-first Copper Cardinal,* laid out in a square. The longest of the linear Copper Cardinals has 67 units.

16. *Trabum*
New York 1977
Douglas fir
9-unit solid stack, 3 tiers of 3 timbers
each alternating
12" x 12" x 36" each
36" x 36" x 36" overall
The artist

This work, with its three rows of three stacked timbers, seems a logical, if belated, conclusion to the artist's Element Series. The solid, closed cubic form makes it one of Andre's most austere works in wood. The title is the possessive plural of *trabs,* Latin for beam, log or timber. A related work, *Pyre* (see page 24) was included in the original 1960 designs for the series. Despite its simple criblike structure of four pairs of stacked timbers, *Pyre* is visually more complex, due to its alternating apertures. Its four-layered, cubic form has an ambiguous interior space, which, being mostly visible, is almost as much "outside" as it is "inside." These works were inspired in part by the artist's memory of ceremonial structures built each year from discarded railroad ties by the Quincy, Massachusetts, fire department, which set them ablaze to celebrate Fourth of July eve.

Walnut Vaudeville, 1978, Douglas fir, 36" x 36" x 39! Installation in Cincinnati, Ohio.

CHRONOLOGY

1935	Born in Quincy, Massachusetts.
1941-50	Educated at Quincy public schools.
1951-53	Attended Phillips Academy, Andover, Massachusetts; met Hollis Frampton and Michael Chapman; studied art with Patrick and Maud Morgan.
1954	Worked at Boston Gear Works, Quincy; traveled to England and France.
1955-56	Served in US Army in North Carolina.
1957-58	Renewed acquaintance with Michael Chapman; worked as editorial assistant for book publisher.
1958-59	Renewed acquaintance with Hollis Frampton; met Frank Stella; cut sculpture in Frank Stella's studio.
1960	*Pyramids* completed; Element Series proposed; works refused by private galleries, collectors and museums.
1960-64	Worked on Pennsylvania Railroad as freight brakeman and conductor in New Jersey; most sculptures lost or destroyed.
1964	Invited by E.C. Goossen to remake *Pyramid* for show at Hudson River Museum, Yonkers, New York and Bennington College, Vermont; first public exhibition.
1965	Invited by Henry Geldzahler to show work in "Shape and Structure," Tibor de Nagy Gallery, New York City; first public exhibition in New York City.

ONE-MAN GALLERY EXHIBITIONS

1965	Tibor de Nagy Gallery, New York
1966	Tibor de Nagy Gallery, New York
1967	Dwan Gallery, Los Angeles Dwan Gallery, New York Konrad Fischer Gallery, Düsseldorf
1968	Heiner Friedrich Gallery, Munich Wide White Space, Antwerp Irving Blum Gallery, Los Angeles
1969	Konrad Fischer Gallery, Düsseldorf Dwan Gallery, New York Wide White Space, Antwerp Gian Enzo Sperone Gallery, Turin
1970	Ace Gallery, Los Angeles

1971	Dwan Gallery, New York
	Locksley-Shea Gallery, Minneapolis
	Konrad Fischer Gallery, Düsseldorf
	Galerie Yvon Lambert, Paris
	Wide White Space, Antwerp
	Heiner Friedrich Gallery, Munich
1972	John Weber Gallery, New York
	Janie C. Lee Gallery, Dallas
	Lisson Gallery, London
	Konrad Fischer Gallery, Düsseldorf
1973	Max Protetch Gallery, Washington, D.C.
	Konrad Fischer Gallery, Düsseldorf
	John Weber Gallery, New York
	Gian Enzo Sperone Gallery, Turin
1974	Wide White Space, Antwerp and Brussels
	Konrad Fischer Gallery, Düsseldorf
	Ace Gallery, Vancouver, British Columbia
1975	John Weber Gallery, New York
	Barbara Cusack Gallery, Houston
	Lisson Gallery, London
	Gian Enzo Sperone Gallery, Rome
	Sperone Westwater Fischer, New York
	Ace Gallery, Vancouver, British Columbia
	Dan Weinberg Gallery, San Francisco
1976	John Weber Gallery, New York
	Barbara Cusack Gallery, Houston
	Ace Gallery, Los Angeles and Venice, California
	Konrad Fischer Gallery, Düsseldorf
	Galerie Yvon Lambert, Paris
1977	Sperone Westwater Fischer, New York
1978	Sperone Westwater Fischer, New York

ONE-MAN MUSEUM AND KUNSTHALLE EXHIBITIONS

1968	Städtisches Museum, Mönchengladbach, West Germany
1969	Gemeentemuseum, The Hague, The Netherlands
1970	The Solomon R. Guggenheim Museum, New York
1971	The St. Louis Art Museum, Missouri
1972	Friends of Contemporary Art, Denver, Colorado
1973	Portland Center for the Visual Arts, Oregon
	Institute of Contemporary Art, Boston
	Addison Gallery of American Art, Andover, Massachusetts
	Thayer Academy, Braintree, Massachusetts
	"Projects" Series, The Museum of Modern Art, New York

1975	Kunsthalle Bern, Switzerland
	The Museum of Modern Art, Oxford, England
1976	Davison Art Center, Wesleyan University, Middletown, Connecticut
	The Clocktower, New York
	Installation of *Prime Terrane,* Detroit Institute of Arts
	Kabinett für Aktuelle Kunst, Bremerhaven, West Germany
	Minneapolis College of Art and Design, Minnesota
1977	Otis Art Institute, Los Angeles
	Joseloff Gallery, Hartford Art School, Connecticut
1978	Whitechapel Art Gallery, London

SELECTED GROUP EXHIBITIONS

1964	"Eight Young Artists," The Hudson River Museum, Yonkers, New York and Bennington College, Vermont. Catalogue with essay by E.C. Goossen.
1965	"Shape and Structure," Tibor de Nagy Gallery, New York. Checklist.
1966	"Primary Structures: Younger American and British Sculptors," The Jewish Museum, New York. Catalogue with text by Kynaston L. McShine.
	"Multiplicity," Institute of Contemporary Art, Boston. Catalogue.
	"10," Dwan Gallery, New York and Los Angeles. Catalogue.
1967	"Scale Models and Drawings," Dwan Gallery, New York.
	"Monuments, Tombstones and Trophies," Museum of Contemporary Crafts, New York.
	"American Sculpture of the Sixties," Los Angeles County Museum of Art (traveled to Philadelphia). Catalogue.
	"Language to be Looked at and/or Things to be Read," Dwan Gallery, New York.
	"A Romantic Minimalism," Institute of Contemporary Art, Philadelphia. Catalogue with introduction by Stephen Prokopoff.
	"Normal Art," Lannis Museum of Normal Art, New York.
	"Art in Series," Finch College Museum of Art, New York.
1968	"Cool Art — 1967," Aldrich Museum of Contemporary Art, Ridgefield, Connecticut. Catalogue.
	"Carl Andre/Robert Barry/Lawrence Weiner," Bradford Junior College, Massachusetts.
	"Minimal Art," Gemeentemuseum, The Hague, The Netherlands (traveled to Düsseldorf and Berlin). Catologue with introduction by Enno Develing and essay by Lucy R. Lippard.
	"3 Blind Mice/de Collecties: Vissers, Peeter, Becht," Stedelijk van Abbemuseum, Eindhoven, The Netherlands. Catalogue.
	"Exterior Situations," Windham College, Putney, Vermont.
	"Language II," Dwan Gallery, New York.
	"Directions 1: Options," Milwaukee Art Center, Wisconsin. Catalogue.

"Art of the Real: USA 1948-1968," The Museum of Modern Art,
New York (traveled to Paris, Zurich, and London). Catalogue with
text by E.C. Goossen.

"Prospect 68," Städtische Kunsthalle, Düsseldorf, West Germany.
Catalogue.

"Earthworks," Dwan Gallery, New York.

"Sammlung 1968 Karl Ströher," Neue Pinakotheka, Munich (traveled
to Hamburg, Berlin, Düsseldorf, and Bern). Catalogue.

"documenta 4," Kassel, West Germany. Catalogue.

1969   "When Attitudes Become Form." Kunsthalle, Bern, (traveled to London,
Krefeld, West Germany). Catalogue.

"Op Losse Schroeven," Stedelijk Museum, Amsterdam. Catalogue.

"Andre, Flavin, Judd, LeWitt and Morris," Hetzel Union Building Gallery,
Pennsylvania State University, University Park. Catalogue with text
by Ira Licht.

"Anti-Illusion: Procedures/Materials," Whitney Museum of American
Art, New York. Catalogue with essays by James Monte and
Marcia Tucker.

"555,087," Seattle Art Museum, Washington. Catalogue with essay
by Lucy R. Lippard.

"Five Sculptors: Andre, Flavin, Judd, Morris, Serra," Art Gallery,
University of California, Irvine. Catalogue.

"Language III," Dwan Gallery, New York.

1970   "Art in Process IV," Finch College Museum of Art, New York. Catalogue.

"Sixty-ninth American Exhibition," The Art Institute of Chicago.
Catalogue.

"Language IV," Dwan Gallery, New York.

"Information," The Museum of Modern Art, New York. Catalogue with
essay by Kynaston L. McShine.

"L'Art Vivant aux Etats-Unis," Foundation Maeght, Saint-Paul-de-Vence,
France. Catalogue with essay by Dore Ashton.

"Between Man and Matter," Tenth Biennale, Tokyo Metropolitan Art
Gallery (traveled to Kyoto and Nagoyo). Catalogue.

"955,000," Vancouver Art Gallery, British Columbia, Canada.
Catalogue.

"1970 Annual Exhibition: Contemporary American Sculpture," Whitney
Museum of American Art, New York. Catalogue.

"Unitary Forms: Minimal Sculpture by Carl Andre, Don Judd, John
McCracken, Tony Smith," San Francisco Museum of Art.
Catalogue with text by Suzanne Foley.

"Five Artists in Five Rooms," Kunstverein, Wuppertal, West Germany,
Catalogue.

"Bildnerische Ausdrucksformen, Sammlung Karl Ströher," Hessisches
Landesmuseum, Darmstadt, West Germany.

1971   "Second Indian Triennial," New Delhi, India. Catalogue.

"Sonsbeek '71," Arnhem, The Netherlands. Two catalogues.

"Guggenheim International Exhibition," Solomon R. Guggenheim
Museum, New York. Catalogue with essays by Edward F. Fry
and Diane Waldman.

1972   "Grids," Institute of Contemporary Art, Philadelphia. Catalogue with
essay by Lucy R. Lippard.

"Actualité d'un Bilan," Galerie Yvon Lambert, Paris. Catalogue with text by Michel Claura and René Denizot.

"Drawings and Diagrams," Rijksmuseum Kröller-Müller, Otterlo, The Netherlands (traveled to Basel and Stuttgart). Catalogue with essay by Carter Ratcliff.

1973   "1973 Biennial Exhibition: Contemporary American Art," Whitney Museum of American Art, New York. Catalogue.

"3D into 2D: Drawing for Sculpture," New York Cultural Center, New York. Catalogue with essay by Susan Ginsberg.

"Bilder, Objeckte, Filme, Konzepte: Herbig Collection," Städtische Galerie im Lenbachhaus, Munich. Catalogue.

"American Art: Third Quarter Century," Seattle Art Museum, Washington. Catalogue with text by Jan van der Marck.

"Contemporanea," Parcheggio di Villa Borghese, Rome. Catalogue.

"Artists' Books," Moore College of Art, Philadelphia. Catalogue.

1974   "Andre/Broodthaers/Buren/Burgin/Gilbert and George/On Kawara/Long/Richter," Palais des Beaux Arts, Brussels, Belgium. Catalogue.

"Some Recent American Art," National Gallery of Victoria, Melbourne, Australia (traveled to Perth, Sydney, Adelaide, Auckland). Catalogue with introduction by Jennifer Licht.

"Tenth Anniversary Exhibition," The Aldrich Museum of Contemporary Art, Ridgefield, Connecticut. Catalogue.

"Sandra and Breck Caldwell Collection," University Art Museum, University of California, Berkeley. Catalogue with text by Brenda Richardson.

1975   "Masterworks in Wood: The Twentieth Century," Portland Art Museum, Oregon. Catalogue with introduction by Jan van der Marck.

"The Condition of Sculpture: A Selection of Recent Sculpture by Younger British and Foreign Artists," Hayward Gallery, London. Catalogue with introduction by William Tucker.

"Sculpture: American Directions 1945-75," National Collection of Fine Arts, Washington, D.C. (traveled to Dallas). Catalogue.

"Painting, Drawing and Sculpture in the '60s and '70s from the Herbert and Dorothy Vogel Collection," Institute of Contemporary Art, Philadelphia (traveled to Cincinnati). Catalogue with introduction by Suzanne Delehanty.

"Functions of Drawing (Drawings from the Collection of Mia and Martin Visser and Geert Jan Visser)," Rijksmuseum Kröller-Müller, Otterlo, The Netherlands (traveled to Basel). Catalogue with introduction by R.H. Fuchs.

"Je/Nous," Musée d'Ixelles, Brussels. Catalogue.

1976   "Drawing Now," The Museum of Modern Art, New York (traveled to Zurich, Baden-Baden, Vienna, Oslo and Tel Aviv). Catalogue with essay by Bernice Rose.

"Seventy-second American Exhibition," The Art Institute of Chicago. Catalogue with introduction by A. James Speyer and essay by Anne Rorimer.

"200 Years of American Sculpture," Whitney Museum of American Art, New York. Catalogue.

"Rooms," Institute for Art and Urban Resources, P.S. 1, Long Island City, New York. Catalogue.

"New York—Downtown Manhattan: SoHo," Akademie der Künste, Berlin. Catalogue.

"Carl Andre, Richard Long and Barry LeVa," Corcoran Gallery,
Washington, D.C. Catalogue with introduction by Jane Livingston.
"Raume," Städtisches Museum, Mönchengladbach, West Germany.
Catalogue with introduction by Johannes Cladders.
"Three Decades of American Art," Seibu Department Store Art
Gallery, Tokyo.

1977   "Woodworks," Nassau County Museum of Art, Roslyn, New York.
Catalogue with essay by Jean E. Feinberg.
"Paris-New York," Musée National d'Art Moderne, Centre Georges
Pompidou, Paris. Catalogue.
"View of a Decade," Museum of Contemporary Art, Chicago.
Catalogue.
"Skulptur Ausstellung in Münster," Westfälisches Landesmuseum für
Kunst und Kulturgeschichte, Münster, West Germany. Catalogue
with introduction by Kasper Koenig and essay by Laszlo Glozer.
"American Drawn and Matched," The Museum of Modern Art,
New York.
"New York: The State of Art," New York State Museum, Albany, New
York. Catalogue with essay by Thomas B. Hess.
"Miniature," Fine Arts Gallery, California State University, Los Angeles.
Catalogue with essay by Sandy Ballatore.
"Works from the Collection of Dorothy and Herbert Vogel," University
of Michigan Art Museum, Ann Arbor. Catalogue with text by
Bret Waller.

1978   "Numerals 1924-1977," Leo Castelli Gallery, New York (traveled
throughout the U.S.). Catalogue with essay by Rainer F. Crone
and entries by Yale University students.

BIBLIOGRAPHY

I. Statements and writings by the artist (entries arranged chronologically).

"Frank Stella," *Allen Memorial Art Museum Bulletin,* Vol. 17, No. 1, Fall 1959, pp. 18-19.

"Preface to Stripe Painting (Frank Stella)," *16 Americans,* New York, The Museum of Modern Art, 1959, p. 76.

First Five Poems, New York, 1961.

"beam . . . room," *Primary Structures: Younger American and British Sculptors,* New York, The Jewish Museum, 1966.

"Art is what we do. Culture is what is done to us" in "Sensibility of the Sixties," *Art in America,* Vol. 55, No. 1, January-February 1967, p. 49. Barbara Rose and Irving Sandler, eds.

"New in New York: Line Work," *Arts Magazine,* Vol. 41, No. 7, May 1967, pp. 49-50. Incorporating statements by Brice Marden, Paul Mogensen and David Novros.

"Artist Interviews Himself," *Carl Andre,* Mönchengladbach, West Germany, Städtisches Museum, 1968.

Andre-Barry-Huebler-Kosuth-LeWitt-Morris-Weiner, [The Xerox Book], New York, Seth Siegelaub/Jack Wendler, 1968.

"Flags: An Opera for Three Voices," *Studio International,* Vol. 177, No. 910, April 1969, pp. 176-177.

Seven Books of Poetry, New York, Dwan Gallery and Seth Siegelaub, 1969. A uniform manuscript edition of 36 signed and numbered sets: *Passport,* 1960; *Shape and Structure,* 1960-65; *A Theory of Poetry,* 1960-65; *One Hundred Sonnets,* 1963; *American Drill,* 1963-68; *Three Operas,* 1964; *Lyrics and Odes,* 1969.

"A Reasonable & Practical Proposal for Artists Who Wish to Remain Free Men in These Terrible Times," *Open Hearing: Art Workers Coalition,* New York, 1969, p. 12.

"Questions et résponses," *VH 101,* No. 1, Spring 1970, pp. 104-107.

Statement in "The Artist and Politics: A Symposium," *Artforum,* Vol. 9, No. 1, September 1970, pp. 35-49.

"A Juror's Statement," *Centennial Exhibition,* San Francisco, San Francisco Art Institute, 1971, np.

Attica Book, New York, Black Emergency Coalition and Writers Protest Against the War in Vietnam, 1972, p. 45. Benny Andrews and Rudolf Baranik, eds.

"Letters," *Artforum,* Vol. 10, No. 7, March 1972, p. 6.

"A Note on Bernhard and Hilla Becher," *Artforum,* Vol. 11, No. 4, December 1972, pp. 59-61.

Quincy Book, Andover, Massachusetts, Addison Gallery of American Art, 1973.

144 Blocks and Stones, Portland, Oregon, Portland Center for the Visual Arts, 1973.

Statement in *Deurle 11/7/73,* Brussels, Belgium, MTL, 1973.

Eleven Poems, Turin, Italy, Gian Enzo Sperone, 1974.

"Against Duchamp," *Praxis,* Vol. 1, No. 1, Spring 1975, p. 115.

"The Role of the Artist in Today's Society," *Art Journal,* Vol. 34, No. 4, Summer 1975, p. 327.

"Eight Statements (on Matisse)," *Art in America,* Vol. 63, No. 4, July-August 1975, pp. 70-71. Jean-Claude Lebensztejn, ed.

"Three Dialogues on Photography," *Interfunktionen,* No. 12, 1975, pp. 1-12. With Hollis Frampton.

"Versions of Witness: A Note on Sculpture and Scholarship," *Art Journal,* Vol. 35, No. 2, Winter 1975-76, pp. 126-127.

"Billy Builder, or The Painfull Machine," chapters I-IV, *Tracks,* Vol. 2, No. 2, Spring 1976, pp. 71-76.

"Billy Builder, or The Painfull Machine," chapters V-XI, *Tracks,* Vol. 2, No. 3, Fall 1976, pp. 53-67.

Statement in Gerritt Henry's "Views from the Studio," *Art News,* Vol. 75, No. 5, May 1976, p. 33.

Public Notice, *Artforum,* Vol. 14, No. 8, April 1976, p. 80.

"Letters," *Artforum,* Vol. 14, No. 9, May 1976, p. 9.

"Correspondence," *Studio International,* Vol. 191, No. 981, May-June 1976, p. 311.

"Commodity and Contradiction, or Contradiction as Commodity," *October,* No. 2, Summer 1976, pp. 100-104. With Jeremy Gilbert-Rolfe.

"Letters," *Art in America,* Vol. 64, No. 5, September-October, 1976, p. 5.

"The bricks abstract: a compilation by Carl Andre," *Art Monthly,* No. 1, October 1976, p. 25.

"From Commentaries: 'The Hanging of John Brown', 'Duty of Water: Arshile Gorky,' 'A Memorial to After Ages'," *Big Deal,* No. 4, Fall 1976, pp. 124-137.

"Questions: Public? Sculpture? For Münster?" *Skulptur Ausstellung in Münster,* Münster, West Germany, Westfälisches Landesmuseum für Kunst und Kulturgeschichte, 1977.

"Billy Builder, or The Painfull Machine," chapters XII-XVI, *Tracks,* Vol. 3, No. 1 and 2, Spring 1977, pp. 145-157.

Statement in "The 20th-Century Artists Most Admired by Other Artists," *Art News,* Vol. 76, No. 9, November 1977, p. 80.

Statement in *Rooms P.S. 1,* New York, Institute for Art and Urban Resources, Inc., 1977.

II. Interviews (entries arranged chronologically)

Tuchman, Phyllis, "An Interview with Carl Andre," *Artforum,* Vol. 8, No. 6, June 1970, pp. 55-61.

Sharp, Willoughby, "Carl Andre," *Avalanche,* No. 1, Fall 1970, pp. 18-27.

Cummings, Paul, "Taped Interview with Carl Andre," Archives of American Art, 1972.

Oliva, Achille Bonito, "Interview with Carl Andre," *Domus,* No. 515, October 1972, pp. 51-52.

Gould, Andrea, "Dialogues with Carl Andre," *Arts Magazine,* Vol. 48, No. 8, May 1974, pp. 27-28.

Lebeer, Irmeline, "Carl Andre," *L'Art Vivant,* No. 50, June 1974, pp. 10-13.

Ballou, Michael and Morgenstern, George, "An Interview with Carl Andre," Minneapolis College of Art and Design newspaper, 1976, pp. 1, 4, 8.

Fuller, Peter, "Carl Andre," *Art Monthly,* No. 16, April, 1978.

III. Books (entries arranged alphabetically; asterisks indicate monograph on the artist)

Anderson, Wayne, *American Sculpture in Process: 1930/1970,* Boston, New York Graphic Society, 1975.

Battcock, Gregory, ed., *Minimal Art, A Critical Anthology,* New York, E.P. Dutton & Co., 1968.

_____,"The Progress of Realism," *Why Art,* New York, E.P. Dutton & Co., 1977.

Burnham, Jack, *The Structure of Art,* New York, Braziller, 1970.

Celant, Germano, *Art Povera,* New York, Praeger Publishers, 1969.

_____, *Senza titolo 1974,* Rome, Balzoni Editore, 1976.

*Develing, Enno, *Carl Andre,* The Hague, The Netherlands, Gemeentemuseum, 1969, reprinted 1974. Includes letter to Develing from Hollis Frampton, excerpts from "Andre: Artist of Transportation" and transcript of symposium at Windham College, Putney, Vermont.

Gorgoni, Gianfranco and Müller, Gregoire, *The new avant garde: Issues for the Art of the Seventies,* New York, Praeger Publishers, 1972.

Hunter, Sam with Jacobus, John, *Modern Art From Post Impressionism to the Present,* New York, Harry N. Abrams, 1976.

Krauss, Rosalind E., *Passages in Modern Sculpture,* New York, The Viking Press, 1977.

Lang, Elizabeth and Tighe, Mary Ann, *Art America,* New York, McGraw Hill, Inc. 1977.

Lippard, Lucy R., *Changing,* New York, E.P. Dutton & Co., 1971.

_____, *Six Years . . . ,* New York, Praeger Publishers, 1973.

Rose, Barbara, *American Art Since 1900,* New York, 2nd edition, Praeger Publishers, 1975.

*Serota, Nicholas, *Carl Andre Sculpture 1959-1977,* London, Whitechapel Art Gallery, 1978.

Vries, Gerd de, ed., *Uber Kunst-On Art: Artists' writings on the changed notion of art after 1965,* Cologne, West Germany, Dumont Schauberg, 1974.

*Waldman, Diane, *Carl Andre,* New York, Solomon R. Guggenheim Museum, 1970.

*Westwater, Angela, ed., *Carl Andre Sculpture 1958-1974,* Bern, Switzerland, Kunsthalle Bern, 1975.

IV. Newspapers and Periodicals (entries arranged chronologically)

Rose, Barbara, "Looking at American Sculpture," *Artforum,* Vol. 3, No. 5, February 1965, pp. 29-36.

Lippard, Lucy, "New York Letter," *Art International,* Vol. 9, No. 6, September 1965, pp. 58-59 (review).

Rose, Barbara, "ABC Art," *Art in America,* Vol. 53, No. 5, October-November 1965, pp. 57-69.

Richard, John, "The Art Shops, The Cool School," *The Sunday Times* (London), February 13, 1966, pp. 28-31.

Bochner, Mel, "Primary Structures," *Arts Magazine,* Vol. 40, No. 8, June 1966, pp. 32-35.

Bourdon, David, "Our Period Style," *Art and Artists,* Vol. 1, No. 3, June 1966, pp. 54-55.

_____, "The Razed Sites of Carl Andre," *Artforum,* Vol. 5, No. 2, October 1966, pp. 14-17.

Lippard, Lucy, "Rejective Art," *Art International,* Vol. 10, No. 8, October 1966, pp. 33-36.

Morris, Robert, "Notes on Sculpture, Part Two," *Artforum,* Vol. 5, No. 2, October 1966, pp. 20-23.

Bannard, Darby, "Present-Day Art and Ready-Made Styles," *Artforum,* Vol. 5, No. 4, December 1966, pp. 30-35.

Michelson, Annette, "10 x 10," *Artforum,* Vol. 5, No. 5, January 1967, pp. 30-31.

Perreault, John, "A Minimal Future? Union-Made, Report on a Phenomenon," *Arts Magazine,* Vol. 41, No. 5, March 1967, pp. 26-31.

Graham, Dan, "A Minimal Future? Models and Monuments," *Arts Magazine,* Vol. 41, No. 5, March 1967, p. 32.

Rose, Barbara, "Shall We Have a Renaissance?" *Art in America,* Vol. 55, No. 2, March-April 1967, p. 31.

Greenberg, Clement, "Recentness of Sculpture," *Art International,* Vol. 11, No. 4, April 1967, p. 19.

Livingston, Jane, "Los Angeles," *Artforum,* Vol. 51, No. 9, May 1967, pp. 62-63 (review).

Smithson, Robert, "Towards the Development of an Air Terminal Site," *Artforum,* Vol. 5, No. 10, June 1967, p. 37.

Fried, Michael, "Art and Objecthood," *Artforum,* Vol. 5, No. 10, Summer 1967, p. 15.

Lippard, Lucy, "Rebelliously Romantic?" *The New York Times,* June 4, 1967, II, p. 25.

Morris, Robert, "Notes on Sculpture, Part Three," *Artforum,* Vol. 5, No. 10, Summer 1967, pp. 24-29.

Bochner, Mel, "Serial Art Systems: Solipsism," *Arts Magazine,* Vol. 41, No. 8, Summer 1967, p. 24.

Davis, Douglas M., "The Dimensions of the Mini-arts," *Art in America,* Vol. 55, No. 6, November-December 1967, p. 85.

Graham, Dan, "Carl Andre," *Arts Magazine,* Vol. 42, No. 4, January 1968, pp. 34-35.

Develing, Enno, "Ideologische Kunst: Minimal Art," *Museumjournaal,* Serie 13, No. 1, 1968, p. 2.

Gilardi, Piero, "Da Londra E. Dusseldorf," *Flash Art,* January 15-February 15, 1968, p. 2.

Chandler, John and Lippard, Lucy R., "The Dematerialization of Art," *Art International,* Vol. 12, No. 2, March 1968, pp. 21-27.

Mellow, James R., "New York Letter," *Art International,* Vol. 12, No. 2, February 1968, p. 73 (review).

Smithson, Robert, "A Museum of Language in the Vicinity of Art," *Art International,* Vol. 12, No. 3, March 1968, pp. 21-27.

Van Schaardenburg, Lieneke, "Carl Andre: Ik Wil Uit De Tijd Sijn," *Vrij Nederland,* April 27, 1968, p. 12.

"Austellungen in New York," *Das Kunstwerk,* Vol. XX, Nos. 6-7, April-May 1968, pp. 23-28.

Blok, C., "Minimal Art at The Hague," *Art International,* Vol. 12, No. 5, May 1968, pp. 18-24.

Nylen, Leif, "Carl Andre," *Paletten,* No. 3, 1968, p. 28.

Gust, Dodie, "Andre: Artist of Transportation," *The Aspen Times,* July 18, 1968, B, p. 3.

Battcock, Gregory, "The Art of the Real," *Arts Magazine,* Vol. 42, No. 8, Summer 1968, p. 44.

Burnham, Jack, "Systems Esthetics," *Artforum,* Vol. 7, No. 1, September 1968, p. 34.

Smithson, Robert, "A Sedimentation of the Mind: Earth Projects," *Artforum,* Vol. 7, No. 1, September 1968, p. 44.

Gilardi, Piero, "Primary Energy and Micro-emotive Artists," *Arts Magazine,* Vol. 43, No. 1, September-October 1968, p. 48.

Alloway, Lawrence, "Interfaces and Options," *Arts Magazine,* Vol. 43, No. 1, September-October 1968, p. 28.

Claura, Michel, "Andre," *Lettres Françaises,* No. 1251, October 1968.

Mellow, James, "New York Letter," *Art International,* Vol. 12, No. 8, October 1968, p. 60 (review).

Junker, Howard, "The New Sculpture: Getting Down to the Nitty Gritty," *Saturday Evening Post,* Vol. 241, No. 22, November 1968, pp. 42-47.

Hutchinson, Peter, "Earth in Upheaval, Earthworks and Landscapes," *Arts Magazine,* Vol. 43, No. 2, November 1968, p. 19.

Chandler, John, "The Last Word in Graphic Art," *Art International,* Vol. 12, No. 9, November 1968, p. 25.

Pleynet, Marcelin, "Peinture et 'Structuralisme'," *Art International,* Vol. 12, No. 9, November 1968, p. 31.

Tillim, Sidney, "Earthworks and the New Picturesque," *Artforum,* Vol. 7, No. 4, December 1968, p. 82.

Rose, Barbara, "Problems of Criticism V, Politics of Art, Part II," *Artforum,* Vol. 7, No. 5, January 1969, pp. 44-49.

Müller, Gregoire, "In the Parisian Desert," *Arts Magazine,* Vol. 43, No. 3, December 1968-January 1969, p. 52.

Develing, Enno, "Kunst En Omgeving (Art and Environment)," *Museumjournaal,* Serie 14, No. 1, 1969, p. 2.

Kramer, Hilton, "The Emperor's New Bikini," *Art in America,* Vol. 57, No. 1, January-February 1969, pp. 49-55.

Meadmore, Clement, "Thoughts on Earthworks, Random Distribution, Softness, Horizontality and Gravity," *Arts Magazine,* Vol. 43, No. 4, February 1969, pp. 26-28.

Armstrong, Lois D., "Los Angeles," *Art News,* Vol. 67, No. 9, February 1969, p. 55 (review).

Reise, Barbara, "Untitled 1969: a Footnote on Art and Minimal-stylehood," *Studio International,* Vol. 177, No. 910, April 1969, pp. 166-172.

Morris, Robert, "Notes on Sculpture, Part Four: Beyond Objects," *Artforum,* Vol. 7, No. 8, April 1969, pp. 50-54.

Amman, Jean Christophe, "Schweizer Brief," *Art International,* Vol. 13, No. 5, May 1969, p. 49 (review).

Blok, C., "Letter from Holland," *Art International,* Vol. 13, No. 5, May 1969, p. 52 (review).

"Carl Andre: Form, Structure, Place," *Arts Magazine,* Vol. 43, No. 7, May 1969, pp. 24-25.

Leider, Philip, "'To Introduce a New Kind of Truth'," *The New York Times,* May 25, 1969, II, p. 41.

Perreault, John, "Art," *The Village Voice,* May 29, 1969, p. 14.

Glueck, Grace, "New York Gallery Notes: Like a Beginning," *Art in America,* Vol. 57, No. 3, May-June 1969, pp. 116-118 (review).

"Reviews and Previews," *Art News,* Vol. 68, No. 4, Summer 1969, p. 12.

Schjeldahl, Peter, "New York Letter," *Art International,* Vol. 13, No. 7, September 1969, p. 71 (review).

Harrison, Charles, "Against Precedents," *Studio International,* Vol. 178, No. 914, September 1969, p. 90.

Alloway, Lawrence, "The Expanding and Disappearing Work of Art," *Auction,* Vol. III, No. 2, October 1969, p. 35.

Trini, Tommaso, "The Prodigal Maker's Trilogy," *Domus,* 478, September 1969, p. 47.

Lippard, Lucy R., "Time: A Panel Discussion," *Art International,* Vol. 13, No. 6, November 1969, pp. 20-23, 39.

Kosuth, Joseph, "Art After Philosophy Part II: Conceptual Art and Recent Art," *Studio International,* Vol. 178, No. 916, November 1969, pp. 160-161.

Davenport, Guy, "Book Review," *Life Magazine,* Vol. 67, No. 24, December 12, 1969, p. 22.

Staber, Margit, "Prospecta-Kunstmarkt 1969," *Art International,* Vol. 14, No. 1, January 1970, p. 65.

Rosenberg, Harold, "The Art World," *The New Yorker,* Vol. 45, No. 51, February 1970, p. 82.

Burnham, Jack, "Alice's Head, Reflections on Conceptual Art," *Artforum,* Vol. 8, No. 6, February 1970, pp. 37-43.

Leider, Philip, "New York," *Artforum*, Vol. 8, No. 6, February 1970. p. 69 (review).

Battcock, Gregory, "The Politics of Space," *Arts Magazine*, Vol. 44, No. 4, February 1970, p. 40.

Bonin, Wibke von, "Germany, the American Presence," *Arts Magazine*, Vol. 44, No. 5, March 1970, p. 65.

"Sheep's Clothing," *Studio International*, Vol. 179, No. 920, March 1970, p. 1.

Henric, Jacques, "Lettre de Paris," *Art International*, Vol. 69, No. 6, April 1970, pp. 54-55 (review).

Leider, Philip, "Literalism and Abstraction: Frank Stella's Retrospective at the Modern," *Artforum*, Vol. 8, No. 8, April 1970, pp. 44-51.

Picard, Lil, "Protest and Rebellion: The Function of the Art Workers Coalition," *Arts Magazine*, Vol. 44, No. 7, May 1970, pp. 18-20.

Nemser, Cindy, "An Interview with Eva Hesse," *Artforum*, Vol. 8, No. 9, May 1970, pp. 59-63.

Sharp, Willoughby, "New Directions in California Sculpture," *Arts Magazine*, Vol. 44, No. 8, Summer 1970, p. 35.

_____, "Los Angeles Galleries," *Arts Magazine*, Vol. 44, No. 8, Summer 1970, p. 50 (review).

Baker, Elizabeth C., "Traveling Ideas: Germany, England," *Art News*, Vol. 69, No. 4, Summer 1970, p. 40.

Love, Joseph P., "The Tenth Tokyo Biennale of Contemporary Art," *Art International*, Vol. 14, No. 6, Summer 1970, pp. 70-74.

Ashton, Dore, "Intercultural Gaps on the Côte d'Azur: Maeght Foundation Shows American Art," *Arts Magazine*, Vol. 45, No. 1, September-October 1970, pp. 38-41.

Davis, Douglas, "Art 1970: New Blood," *Newsweek*, Vol. 76, No. 14, October 5, 1970, p. 88.

Waldman, Diane, "Holding the Floor," *Art News*, Vol. 69, No. 6, October 1970, p. 60.

Hahn, Otto, "Notes sur L'Avant Garde," *VH 101*, No. 3 Autumn 1970, p. 80.

Kramer, Hilton, "Art: Andre 'Carpets' at the Guggenheim," *The New York Times*, October 3, 1970, p. 25 (review).

Perreault, John, "Art Solutions?" *The Village Voice*, October 8, 1970.

Schjeldahl, Peter, "High Priest of Minimal," *The New York Times*, October 18, 1970, p. 23.

Gruen, John, "Galleries and Museums," *New York Magazine*, October 28, 1970, p. 66 (review).

Dienst, Rolf-Gunter, "L'Art Vivant aux Etats-Unis," *Das Kunstwerk*, Vol. XXIII, Nos. 11-12, October-November 1970, p. 10.

Tuchman, Phyllis, "American Art in Germany: The History of a Phenomenon," *Artforum*, Vol. 9, No. 3, November 1970, pp. 58-69.

Develing, Enno, "Sculpture as Place," *Art and Artists*, Vol. 5, No. 8, November 1970, pp. 18-21.

Rose, Barbara, "Art," *Vogue*, Vol. 156, No. 8, November 1970, p. 57 (review).

Lippard, Lucy R., "The Dilemma," *Arts Magazine*, Vol. 45, No. 2, November 1970, pp. 27-29.

Müller, Gregoire, "Carl Andre at the Guggenheim," *Arts Magazine*, Vol. 45, No. 2, November 1970, p. 57 (review).

Lippard, Lucy R., "The Art Workers Coalition: Not a History," *Studio International*, Vol. 180, No. 927, November 1970, pp. 171-174.

Siegel, Jeanne, "Carl Andre: Artworker," *Studio International*, Vol. 180, no. 927, November 1970, pp. 175-179.

Marandel, J. Patrice, "Lettre de New York," *Art International*, Vol. 14, No. 10, Christmas 1970, pp. 71-74 (review).

Masheck, Joseph, "New York," *Artforum*, Vol. 9, No. 4, December 1970, pp. 78-79 (review).

Hope, Henry R., "Editor's Notebook," *Art Journal*, Vol. 30, No. 2, Winter 1970-71, p. 224.

Develing, Enno, "Carl Andre: art as a social fact," *Artscanada*, Vol. 27, No. 6, December 1970-January 1971, pp. 47-49.

Schwartz, Therese, "The Political Scene," *Arts Magazine*, Vol. 45, No. 3, December 1970-January 1971, p. 16.

Borgeaud, Bernard, "Art Abroad: Paris," *Arts Magazine*, Vol. 45, No. 3, December 1970-January 1971, p. 46.

"Whitney Sculpture? Show," *Pictures on Exhibit*, Vol. XXXIV, No. 4, January 1971, p. 8 (review).

Ratcliff, Carter, "New York Letter," *Art International*, Vol. 15, No. 1, January 1971, p. 29 (review).

Plagens, Peter, "Los Angeles," *Artforum*, Vol. 9, No. 5, January 1971, p. 91 (review).

Battcock, Gregory, "New York Letter: Art as a Communicative Phenomenon," *Art and Artists*, Vol. 5, No. 10, January 1971, p. 64.

Dienst, Rolf-Gunter, "Kolner Kunstmarkt 70," *Das Kunstwerk*, Vol. XXIV, No. 1, January 1971, p. 51.

"Kunst als Kontext," *Interfunktionen*, No. 5, p. 16 and back cover.

Jappe, George, "Konrad Fischer Interviewed," *Studio International*, Vol. 181, No. 930, February 1971, p. 68.

Link Indian Newsmagazine, February 1971, pp. 34-35.

Illustrations, *Flash Art*, February-March 1971, pp. 1, 2.

Schwartz, Therese, "News of the Art World," *Arts Magazine*, Vol. 45, No. 4, February 1971, p. 16.

——————, "The Political Scene," *Arts Magazine*, Vol. 45, No. 5, March 1971, p. 15.

Monte, James, "Looking at the Guggenheim International," *Artforum*, Vol. 9, No. 7, March 1971, pp. 28-30 (review).

"News of the Art World," *Arts Magazine*, Vol. 45, No. 5, March 1971, p. 16.

Green, Denise, "Reviews," *Arts Magazine*, Vol. 45, No. 5, March 1971, p. 52.

Burnham, Jack, "Unveiling the Consort, Part II," *Artforum*, Vol. 9, No. 8, April 1971, p. 48.

Pincus-Witten, Robert, "New York," *Artforum*, Vol. 9, No. 8, April 1971, p. 76 (review).

Perreault, John, "Plaster People . . .," *The Village Voice*, April 22, 1971, p. 25.

Parent, Beatrice, "Land Art," *Opus International*, Vol. 23, March 1971, pp. 22-27.

Rosenstein, Harris, "Reviews and Previews," *Art News*, Vol. 70, No. 3, May 1971, p. 10.

Baker, Elizabeth C., "Editorial," *Art News*, Vol. 70, No. 3, May 1971, p. 25.

Domingo, Willis, "Carl Andre at Dwan," *Arts Magazine*, Vol. 45, No. 7, May 1971, p. 55 (review).

Garcia-Herraiz, E., "Carl Andre, Galeria Dwan," New York, *Goya*, No. 102, May 1971, p. 419 (review).

Davis, Douglas, "Art by the Foot," *Newsweek*, Vol. 77, No. 18, May 31, 1971, pp. 84-85 (review).

Baker, Kenneth, "Carl Andre, Dwan Gallery," *Artforum*, Vol. 9, No. 10, June 1971, pp. 80-81 (review).

Blotkamp, Carel, "Sculpture at Sonsbeek," *Studio International*, Vol. 183, No. 936, September 1971, pp. 70-73.

Linville, Kasha, "Sonsbeek: Speculations, Impressions," *Artforum*, Vol. 10, No. 2, October 1971, p. 55 (review).

Spear, Athena, "Brancusi and Contemporary Sculpture," *Arts Magazine*, Vol. 46, No. 2, November 1971, pp. 28-31.

Venturi, Luca M., "Carl Andre," *Flash Art*, October-November 1971, pp. 4-5.

Perreault, John, "A Healthy Pluralism," *The Vilage Voice*, February 17, 1971, p. 21.

"Reviews and Previews," *Art News*, Vol. 71. No. 1, March 1972, pp. 9-10.

Elderfield, John, "grids," *Artforum*, Vol. 10, No. 9, May 1972, pp. 52-59.

Brett, Guy, "Sculpture Takes Its Own Shape," *The Times* (London), May 11, 1972.

Russell, John, "Resurrection," *The Sunday Times* (London), May 14, 1972.

Cork, Richard, "Art News," *The Evening Standard* (London), May 18, 1972.

Dosling, Nigel, "Married Talents," *The Sunday Observer* (London), May 21, 1972.

Tisdall, Caroline, "Any Old Iron," *Guardian* (London), June 1, 1972.

Vaizey, Marina, "Carl Andre," *The Financial Times* (London), June 7, 1972.

Fuller, Peter, "Carl Andre at Lisson Gallery," *The Connoiseur*, Vol. 180, No. 725, July 1972, p. 237 (review).

Mayer, Rosemary, "Group Show at John Weber," *Arts Magazine*, Vol. 47, No. 3, December 1972-January 1973, p. 76 (review).

ART PRESS, No. 5, December 1972-January 1973, pp. 13, 15.

Levin, Kim, "Eros, Samaras and Recent Art," *Arts Magazine*, Vol. 47, No. 3, December 1972-January 1973, p. 52.

Boice, Bruce, "Reviews," *Artforum*, Vol. 9, No. 5, January 1973, pp. 84-85.

Mayer, Rosemary, "Andre, Haacke, Holt, James, Miller, Obering," *Arts Magazine*, Vol. 47, No. 3, December 1972-January 1973, p. 75.

Marck, Jan van der, "Sculptor Carl Andre Scavenging Materials for New Show," *The Sunday Oregonian* (Portland), February 11, 1973.

Everly, Jack, "Carl Andre Work, Calm, Memorable," *The Sunday Oregonian* (Portland), February 18, 1973.

Halasz, Piri, "Washington: The Politics of Cheese," *Art News*, Vol. 72, No. 3, March 1973, p. 55.

Dyer, Ellen, "Carl Andre: Sculptor, Scavenger in the Scrapyards of Time and Place," *The Patriot Ledger* (Quincy, Mass.), April 12, 1973.

Perreault, John, "Miniatures that Dwarf the Massive," *The Village Voice*, April 26, 1973, p. 34.

Schjeldahl, Peter, "One Takes Away, the Other Piles It On," *The New York Times*, April 29, 1973, II, p. 21.

Marck, Jan van der, "Carl Andre at PCVA," *Art in America,* Vol. 61, No. 3, May-June 1973, pp. 110-112.

Pursor, Edward, "Polemic Preserves," *Art-Rite,* No. 2, Summer 1973, p. 14.

Smith, Roberta, "Reviews," *Artforum,* Vol. 9, No. 10, June 1973, p. 86.

Crimp, Douglas, "New York Letter," *Art International,* Vol. 17, No. 6, Summer 1973, p. 88 (review).

Ashton, Dore, "Principles of Transitoriness," *Studio International,* Vol. 186, No. 958, September 1973, pp. 91-92.

Krauss, Rosalind, "Sense and Sensibility: Reflections on Post '60s Sculpture," *Artforum,* Vol. 12, No. 3, November 1973, pp. 43-53.

Gerson, Françoise de, "L'art conceptuel: Entreprise de déconstruction," *Clés pour les Arts,* No. 40, February 1974, pp. 16-21.

McCaughey, Patrick, "The seriousness of 137 bricks," *The Age,* February 13, 1974 (review).

Thomas, Daniel, "Leaders of the cool school," *The Sydney Morning Herald,* February 15, 1974 (review).

Makin, Jeffrey, "Nothing to say, and saying it," *The Age,* February 15, 1974, p. 28 (review).

McCulloch, Alan, "New ness — but that's all," (Australian newspaper, Sperone Westwater Fischer clipping file) (review).

Whalen, Michele, "American art — or is it?" *The Age,* February 15, 1974.

Shannon, Michael, "If it's in a gallery it must be art," *The Australian,* February 16, 1974 (review).

Alloway, Lawrence, "Artists as Writers, Part Two: The Realm of Language," *Artforum,* Vol. 12, No. 8, April 1974, pp. 30-35.

Thomas, Daniel, "Beauty in the artificiality of Minimal Art," *Sydney Morning Herald,* April 4, 1974.

McGrath, Sandra, "Post-Pollock painters extend art form," *The Australian,* April 6, 1974, p. 25 (review).

Kelly, Frances, "After the empty canvas new US art can be fun," *The National Times,* April 8-13, 1974 (review).

Mignacca, Eneide, "Perplexity in the eyes of the beholder," *National Review,* April 11-18, 1974, p. 14 (review).

Gleeson, James, "The pendulum's swing," *The Sun-Herald,* April 14, 1974 (review).

Borlase, Nancy, "More shadow than substance," *The Bulletin,* April 20, 1974 (review).

"Review," *Heute Kunst,* No. 6, April-May 1974, p. 86.

Gilbert-Rolfe, Jeremy, "Reviews," *Artforum,* Vol. 12, No. 10, June 1974, p. 68.

"Mönchengladbach: 'Sammlung Panza,'" *Magazin Kunst,* No. 2, 1974, p. 28.

Kuspit, Donald B., "Carl Andre at Weber," *Art in America,* Vol. 62, No. 4, July-August 1974, p. 83 (review).

Knott, Laurie, "American art — self-hypnosis or a matter of seeing the unseen," (Perth, Australia newspaper, Sperone Westwater Fischer clipping file) (review).

Oliver, Robin, "Nothing humdrum in this conundrum," (Australian newspaper, Sperone Westwater Fischer clipping file).

"The art of brick-dropping," *The Australian,* June 20, 1974.

Mason, Murray, "Questioning the accepted," *The West Australian,* June 29, 1974 (review).

Baxter, Cedric, "American art? It's 'garbage,'" (Australian newspaper, Sperone Westwater Fischer clipping file), p. 31 (review).

Whittle, Bertram, "Profundity of the house brick," (Australian newspaper, Sperone Westwater Fischer clipping file), p. 32.

Robbins, Jim, "Sees," *The Advertiser,* June 4, 1974.

North, Ian, "A Show with Some Shocks," (Australian newspaper, Sperone Westwater Fischer clipping file) (review).

Kingsley, April, "Carl Andre at John Weber, New York," *Art International,* Vol. 18, No. 6, Summer 1974, p. 45 (review).

Phillpot, Clive, "Feedback," *Studio International,* Vol. 188, No. 969, September 1974, pp. 97-103.

Morris, Lynda, "Projekt 74," *Studio International,* Vol. 188, No. 969, September 1974, pp. 97-103.

Harrison, Charles, "Projekt 74," *Studio International,* Vol. 188, No. 969, September 1974, pp. 97-103.

"Carl Andre," *The Tate Gallery 1972-4 Biennial Report and Illustrated Catalog of Acquisitions,* 1975, pp. 73-75.

Russell, John, "Art: Matrimonial Scenes and Cityscapes," *The New York Times,* January 18, 1975, p. 21.

Alloway, Lawrence, "Art," *The Nation,* February 15, 1975, pp. 189-190.

Lubell, Ellen, "Carl Andre," *Arts Magazine,* Vol. 49, No. 7, March 1975, p. 15 (review).

"Prints and Portfolios Published: Carl Andre," *The Print Collector's Newsletter,* Vol. VI, No. 1, March-April 1975, p. 13.

Smith, Roberta, "Reviews," *Artforum,* Vol. 13, No. 8, April 1975, pp. 73-74.

Martin, Barry, "The Condition of Sculpture," *Studio International,* Vol. 190, No. 976, July-August 1975, pp. 75-76.

Crichton, Fenella, "Carl Andre at Lisson," *Art International,* Vol. 19, No. 7, September 1975, p. 51 (review).

Bourdon, David, "The New Season: Pier Groups," *The Village Voice,* September 8, 1975, pp. 122-124.

Young, Joseph E., "Serial Prints," *The Print Collector's Newsletter,* Vol. VI, No. 4, September-October 1975, pp. 89-93.

"Museums and Dealers' Catalogues," *The Print Collector's Newsletter,* Vol. VI, No. 4, September-October 1975, p. 110.

Morris, Lynda, "Carl Andre Poems 1958-1974," *Studio International,* Vol. 190, No. 977, September-October 1975, pp. 160-161.

Grüterich, Marlis, "Carl Andre: Kunsthalle, Bern," *Studio International,* Vol. 190, No. 977, September-October 1975, pp. 158-159 (review).

Alloway, Lawrence, "Caro's Art-Tucker's Choice," *Artforum,* Vol. 14, No. 2, October 1975, pp. 65-71.

Russell, John, "Review," *The New York Times,* October 4, 1975, p. 15.

Pollock, Duncan, "You Don't Need To See To Believe In Boulder," *Rocky Mountain News* October 19, 1975, p. 30.

Bourdon, David, "Review," *The Village Voice,* October 20, 1975, p. 104.

Russell, John, "Review of 'Projects in Nature,'" *The New York Times,* October 25, 1975, p. 25.

Perry, Art, "In Chips with Giant Blocks," *Province* (Vancouver), November 19, 1975, p. 31.

Lowndes, Joan, "Andre and His Wood Blocks," *The Vancouver Sun,* November 21, 1975.

Dunham, Judith L., "Sculpture as Place," *Artweek,* November 29, 1975, pp. 1, 16.

Grove, Nancy, "Carl Andre," *Arts Magazine,* Vol. 50, No. 4, December 1975, p. 13 (review).

Crary, Jonathan, "Projects in Nature," *Arts Magazine,* Vol. 50, No. 4, December 1975, p. 52.

Patton, Phil, "Carl Andre," *Art News,* Vol. 74, No. 10, December 1975, p. 125 (review).

Seeman, Joan, "The Flowering of American Sculpture," *Art News,* Vol. 74, No. 10, December 1975, pp. 46-48.

Smith, Roberta, "New York," *Artforum,* Vol. 14, No. 5, January 1976, pp. 61-62 (review).

Russell, John, "Gallery View: No Shortage of Artistic Energy in SoHo," *The New York Times,* January 18, 1976, II, p. 30.

——————————, "'Drawing Now,' One of the Modern's Best," *The New York Times,* January 24, 1976, p. 23.

Smith, Roberta, "Reviews," *Artforum,* Vol. 14, No. 5, January 1976, pp. 61-62.

Battcock, Gregory, "Good Taste, Bad Taste: four artists in New York," *Domus,* 555, February 1976, p. 47.

Simpson, Colin, "The Tate Drops a Costly Brick," *The Sunday Times* (London), February 15, 1976.

Lucie-Smith, Edward, "Do We Need Toys Like This At The Tate?" *Evening Standard* (London), February 17, 1976, p. 13.

Semple, Robert B., Jr., "Tate Gallery Buys Pile of Bricks — Or Is It Art?" *The New York Times,* February 20, 1976, p. 35.

Russell, John, "An Andre 'Is What It Is, Not Another Thing,'" *The New York Times,* February 20, 1976, p. 35.

"Tate Gallery Defends Purchase of Bricks," *The Times* (London), p. 3.

Lubell, Ellen, "Carl Andre," *Arts Magazine,* Vol. 50, No. 7, March 1976, p. 16 (review).

"In the Eye of the Beholder," *Washington Star,* February 25, 1976.

Blume, Mary, "Playing the Museum Game Now and Then," *International Herald Tribune,* February 28-29, 1976.

Editorial, *Studio International,* Vol. 191, No. 980, March-April 1976, pp. 94-95.

"2 Sculptors Seek To Withdraw Work From Whitney Show," *The New York Times,* March 31, 1976, II, p. 1.

"T 1534. Untitled. 1966," *Burlington Magazine,* Vol. 118, No. 877, April 1976, pp. 187-188.

Smith, Roberta, "Drawing Now (And Then)," *Artforum,* Vol. 14, No. 8, April 1976, pp. 52-56 (review).

Henry, Gerritt, "Views from the Studio," *Art News,* Vol. 75, No. 5, May 1976, p. 32.

Perrone, Jeff, "Carl Andre: Art Versus Talk," *Artforum,* Vol. 14, No. 9, May 1976, pp. 32-33.

Bourdon, David, "Carl Andre Protests Museological Mutilation," *The Village Voice,* May 31, 1976, p. 117.

Goldberg, Roselee, "Recent Performance Work," *Studio International,* Vol. 191, No. 981, May-June 1976, p. 222.

Hess, Thomas B., "Carl Andre Has The Floor," *New York Magazine,* Vol. 9, No. 7, June 7, 1976, pp. 70-72.

Hoelterhoff, Manuela, "A Little of Everything at the Whitney," *The Wall Street Journal,* June 9, 1976.

Magnusson, Paul, "Horizontal Sculpture is NOT a Patio," *The Detroit Free Press,* June 10, 1976, pp. 3A, 11A.

Colby, Joy, "DIA faces $50,000 Dilemma," *Detroit News,* June 20, 1976, pp. 1H, 11A.

Miro, Marsha, "Patio Blocks Do a Fugue," *Detroit Free Press,* June 20, 1976.

Russell, John, "An Unwanted School in Queens Becomes An Ideal Art Center," *The New York Times,* June 20, 1976, D, p. 41.

Colby, Joy Hakanson, "Artist Labors for Detroit," *The Detroit News,* June 21, 1976, p. 1B.

Rosenberg, Harold, "The Art World: Ideal and Real," *The New Yorker,* Vol. 52, No. 17, June 14, 1976, pp. 80-85.

Wilson, William, "Art Walk," *Los Angeles Times,* July 2, 1976, IV, p. 5.

Ballatore, Sandy, "Carl Andre on Work and Politics," *Artweek,* Vol. 7, No. 24, July 3, 1976, pp. 1 and the last.

Sischy, Ingrid, "200 Years of American Sculpture. (By Armstrong, Craven, Feder, Haskell, Krauss, Robbins, Tucker)," *The Print Collector's Newsletter,* Vol. VII, No. 3, July-August 1976, pp. 92-94.

Krauss, Rosalind, "Las Vegas Comes to the Whitney," *Partisan Review,* Vol. 43, No. 2, 1976, pp. 467-471.

Masheck, Joseph, "The Carpet Paradigm: Critical Prolegomena to a Theory of Flatness," *Arts Magazine,* Vol. 51, No. 1, September 1976, pp. 82-109, (cf. fn 170).

Baldwin, Carl R., "Whitney Flap: More on Artists' 'Moral Rights,'" *Art in America,* Vol. 64, No. 5, September-October 1976, pp. 10-11.

Ahorn, Hannelore, "Skuptur zum Betreten," *Nordsee-Zeitung,* October 13, 1976.

"Carl Andre at MCAD," *Arts* (Minneapolis College of Art and Design), Vol. 1, No. 11, October 1976, p. 6.

Morphet, Richard, "Carl Andre's Bricks," *Burlington Magazine,* Vol. 118, No. 884, November 1976, pp. 762-767.

Marioni, Tom, "Hard Bop," *Vision,* No. 3, November 1976 (Crown Point Press, Oakland, California), pp. 5-21, ills. of Andre's New York works 1958-60, pp. 56-61.

Forgey, Benjamin, "Sculpture That's An Echo, Not a Choice," *The Washington Star,* December 12, 1976, G, pp. 1, 28.

Richard, Paul, "Art: Off the Wall and Onto the Floor," *The Washington Post,* December 12, 1976, F, p. 1, 18.

Cork, Richard, "The message in a brick," *The Evening Standard* (London), December 30, 1976, p. 11.

Cover, *Art-Rite,* No. 14, Winter 1976-77, p. 1.

Larson, Philip, "Carl Andre," *Arts Magazine,* Vol. 51, No. 5, January 1977, p. 10 (review).

Wilson, William, "Four Showings of Minimalisms," *The Los Angeles Times,* February 7, 1977, IV, p. 2.

Tuchman, Phyllis, "Minimalism and Critical Response," *Artforum,* Vol. 15, No. 9, May 1977, pp. 26-31.

Kramer, Hilton, "Sculpture — From Boring to Brilliant," *The New York Times,* May 15, 1977, D, p. 27 (review).

Dunbar, Jill, "Art/Four Shows That Go Beyond Canvas," *The Villager,* May 12, 1977, p. 11.

Packer, William, "Carl Andre's Bricks," *The Financial Times* (London), May 3, 1977.

Wharton, Michael, "Art and no art," *Daily Telegraph* (London), May 14, 1977.

Goldenthal, Jolene, "Art/Sculpture Park for Hartford," *The Hartford Courant,* July 17, 1977, F, p. 2.

Perreault, John, "Outside the City: Lumber in the Woods," *The SoHo Weekly News,* July 21, 1977, pp. 25, 41.

Lang, Joel, "Sculptor Gets Off to Rocky Start With Creation in City," *The Hartford Courant,* August 23, 1977, p. 31.

_____, "Criticisms of Park Art Doesn't Rock Sculptor," *The Hartford Courant,* August 25, 1977, pp. 1, 10.

"Rollicking Rocks," *The Hartford Courant,* August 26, 1977, p. 1.

Pappas, Nancy, "Artist Wins Support Despite Brickbats," *The Hartford Courant,* August 26, 1977, p. 17.

"Are Boulders Art?" *The Hartford Courant,* August 27, 1977, p. 18.

Lohman, Phil, "If It Starts a Trend," *The Hartford Courant,* August 27, 1977, p. 19.

Lang, Joel, "Sculptor Adamant About His Art," *The Hartford Courant,* August 28, 1977.

Russell, John, "Carl Andre, as One Critic Sees Him," *The New York Times,* reprinted, *The Hartford Courant,* August 28, 1977, p. 28.

Lang, Joel, "Sculpture Foes Shaping Plans," *The Hartford Courant,* August 29, 1977.

Martin, Antoinette, "Sculpture's Neighbors Ready to Rock Boat," *The Hartford Courant,* August 29, 1977.

—————————, "Rock Opponents Tighten Stand," *The Hartford Courant,* August 30, 1977, pp. 1, 16.

Seremet, Patricia, "What's Up Roc(ks)?" *West Hartford News,* September 1, 1977, pp. 1, 7.

"A Fable: Us vs. HUD, Or Hartford on the Rocks," *West Hartford News,* September 1, 1977.

Berkman, Florence, "Carl Andre Sculpture: Is It Art? Is It Eloquent?" *West Hartford News,* September 1, 1977.

Pinyoun, Harvey, "The Rock Field," *The First Church of Christ News Letter* (Hartford, Connecticut), September 2, 1977, np.

Russell, John, "Art People," *The New York Times,* September 2, 1977, C, p. 16.

Martin, Antoinette, "Rock Sculpture Fee Hasn't Been Paid," *The Hartford Courant,* September 2, 1977, p. 42.

Keller, Anthony S., "Rocks or Art?" *The Hartford Courant,* September 4, 1977, p. 31.

Goldenthal, Jolene, "Art/Sculptural Place and Space," *The Hartford Courant,* September 2, 1977, F, p. 3.

"Sculpture?" *Bridgeport Sunday Post,* September 4, 1977.

Henry, Diane, "Some Residents of Hartford Are Throwing Stones At Sculptor's Extended 'Serenity of the Graveyard," *The New York Times,* September 5, 1977, p. 21.

Hanson, Bernard, "'Stone Field Sculpture' Providing a Pivot," *Hartford Advocate,* Vol. IV, No. 4, September 14, 1977, pp. 14-15.

Polman, Dick, "Can Hartford Learn To Love Rocks?" *Hartford Advocate,* Vol. IV, No. 4, September 14, 1977, p. 2.

Bourdon, David, "Carl Andre Rocks Hartford," *The Village Voice,* September 19, 1977, p. 79.

Driscoll, Dainey, "Bristol Boulders Used In Hartford Sculpture," *Bristol Press,* September 19, 1977, p. 4.

"Notes on People," *The New York Times,* September 23, 1977, D, p. 19.

Gruen, John, "Tale of Two Cities," *Art News,* Vol. 76, No. 7, September 1977, p. 111, ill. p. 109.

Regan, Michael, "Lawyers Tell City To Pay for Rocks," *The Hartford Courant,* October 12, 1977.

Askey, Ruth, "Contemporary Miniatures," *Artweek,* Vol. 8, No. 35, October 22, 1977, p. 6.

Wilson, William, "'Miniature' Lost in a Cal State L.A. Art Show," *Los Angeles Times,* October 30, 1977, pp. 86, 88.

Robertson, Fyfe, moderator, "Robbie Programme (Art), Transmission: 15th August 1977," radio program transcript published in *Art Monthly,* No. 11, October 1977, p. 8.

Greenberg, Clement, "Looking for the Avant-Garde," *Arts Magazine,* Vol. 52, No. 3, November 1977, p. 87.

Giacomo, Carol, "Andre Traces How He Got Here From There," *The Hartford Courant,* November 4, 1977, p. 35.

Robertson, J. Greg, "Andre Defends Rock Sculpture, Acceptance of $87,000 Fee," *The Hartford Courant,* November 4, 1977, p. 21.

"Andre's square one," *Art News,* Vol. 76, No. 9, November 1977, p. 29.

Glueck, Grace, "The 20th-Century Artists Most Admired by Other Artists," *Art News,* Vol. 76, No. 9, November 1977, pp. 79, 80.

Marzorati, Gerald, "INTERVIEW: lawrence alloway," *Art Workers News,* Vol. 7, No. 2, October 1977, p. 3.

"Present Indicative," *Horizon,* Vol. 20, No. 3, November 1977, p. 59.

Goldenthal, Jolene, "Art/Andre's 'Redoubt' at Joseloff," *The Hartford Courant,* November 13, 1977, G, p. 2.

"The Talk of the Town: Indentations in Space," *The New Yorker,* November 21, 1977, pp. 51-52.

Glueck, Grace, "Art People," *The New York Times,* November 18, 1977, p. C25.

Smith, Robert G., "Sculptor Gets Your Tax $$ for Putting Rocks in Rows," *National Enquirer,* November 22, 1977, p. 37.

Bourdon, David, "Carl Andre," *Arts Magazine,* Vol. 52, No. 4, December 1977, p. 5.

Olmstead, Alan, "Shakespeare, 36 stones and the Park River," *Yankee Magazine,* October 20, 1977.

"Andre 'Rocks' Disturb Hartford," *Artists Equity Association of New York,* October 1977, p. 5.

Smith, Peter, "Illustrations for Art-Language, Art and Language," *Art Monthly,* No. 13, December 1977-January 1978, p. 28.

Bell, Jane, "The $100 Gallery," *Village Voice,* December 26, 1977, p. 71.

Scheible, Sue, "Found going rocky in Hartford," "Owes it all to Quincy," *The Patriot Ledger* (Quincy, Mass.), December 30, 1977, p. 24.

Lippard, Lucy R., "'Wood' at the Nassau County Museum," *Art in America,* Vol. 65, No. 6, November-December 1977, pp. 136-137 (review).

"Sculpture by Carl Andre to be unveiled Saturday," *Citizen Marquee,* January 6, 1978, p. 6.

Taggart, Patrick, "Sculptor's works different," *Austin American-Statesman,* January 9, 1978, C, p. 1.

McIntyre, Mary, "Andre's sculpture utilizes viewer," *Austin American-Statesman,* January 15, 1978, p. 28.

Kelly, Kay, "Carl Andre: Controversial sculptor/poet challenges Occidental sensibilities," *The Daily Texan,* January 16, 1978, p. 4.

"Exhibit of minimal movement art at Hurlbutt Gallery this month," *Greenwich Time,* February 6, 1978, p. 10.

Russell, John, "Art People," *New York Times,* February 17, 1978, C, p. 20.

Willard, L.F., "Would You Pay $87,000 for These 36 Rocks?" *Yankee Magazine,* February 1978, pp. 221-223, 206-209.

Ennis, Michael, "Spilled Sculpture," *Texas Monthly,* March 1978, p. 120.

Findsen, Owen, "Andre, Master of Horizontal Art," *The Cincinnati Enquirer,* March 5, 1978, F, p. 7.

Tuchman, Phyllis, "Background of a Minimalist: Carl Andre," *Artforum,* Vol. 16, No. 7, March 1978, pp. 29-33.

Beatty, Frances, "Aycock, Andre and Stephan in SoHo Shows," *Art/World,* Vol. 2, No. 7, March 15/April 15, 1978, pp. 1, 13.

"Ordinary Material Transformed Into Art," *The Cincinnati Post,* March 11, 1978, p. 28.

Dunbar, Jill, "At the Galleries," *The Villager,* March 16, 1978, p. 16.

Gibb, Francis, "Brick-pile 'sculpture' in one-man show," *The Daily Telegraph* (London), March 16, 1978, p. 10.

"What the public thinks of the artist who makes up shapes like this," *Daily Mail* (London), March 18, 1978, p. 9.

Vaizey, Marina, "The apotheosis of the common brick," *The Sunday Times* (London), March 19, 1978, p 35.

Shepherd, Michael, "Man behind the bricks," *The Sunday Telegraph* (London), March 19, 1978, p. 16.

Overy, Paul, "New meaning for the ordinary," *The Times* (London), March 21, 1978, p. 11.

Kramer, Hilton, "The New Line: Minimalism Is Americanism," *The New York Times,* March 26, 1978, D, p. 29.

Cuts Terrane, 1978, Concrete blocks, 4" x 20' 6" x 40' 4½" overall. Installation at Laguna Gloria Art Museum.